D0761968

Race, Crime, and Punishment

CRIME, JUSTICE, AND PUNISHMENT

Race, Crime, and Punishment

Delores D. Jones-Brown

Austin Sarat, GENERAL EDITOR

CHELSEA HOUSE PUBLISHERS
Philadelphia

Chelsea House Publishers

Editor in Chief Stephen Reginald
Production Manager Pamela Loos
Art Director Sara Davis
Director of Photography Judy L. Hasday
Managing Editor James D. Gallagher
Senior Production Editor LeeAnne Gelletly

Staff for RACE, CRIME, AND PUNISHMENT

Senior Editor John Ziff
Associate Art Director/Designer Takeshi Takahashi
Picture Researcher Patricia Burns
Cover Illustrator Takeshi Takahashi

3 5 7 9 8 6 4 2

The Chelsea House World Wide Web address is
http://www.chelseahouse.com

Library of Congress Cataloging-in-Publication Data

Race, crime, and punishment / Delores D. Jones-Brown
   p. cm. — (Crime, justice, and punishment)
Includes bibliographical references and index.
Summary: Examines the relationship between race and
crime in the United States and the role that race plays in
the American criminal justice system.

ISBN 0-7910-4273-1

1. Crime and race—United States—Juvenile literature. 2.
Discrimination in criminal justice administration—United
States—Juvenile literature. [1. Crime and race. 2. Dis-
crimination in criminal justice administration. 3. Criminal
justice, Administration of.] I. Jones-Brown, Delores D. II.
Series.
HV6197.US R34 2000
364'089'00973—dc21
                                        99-057387

Contents

CRIME, JUSTICE, AND PUNISHMENT

Fears and Fascinations:

An Introduction to
Crime, Justice, and Punishment

By Austin Sarat

We live with crime and images of crime all around us. Crime evokes in most of us a deep aversion, a feeling of profound vulnerability, but it also evokes an equally deep fascination. Today, in major American cities the fear of crime is a major fact of life, some would say a disproportionate response to the realities of crime. Yet the fear of crime is real, palpable in the quickened steps and furtive glances of people walking down darkened streets. At the same time, we eagerly follow crime stories on television and in movies. We watch with a "who done it" curiosity, eager to see the illicit deed done, the investigation undertaken, the miscreant brought to justice and given his just deserts. On the streets the presence of crime is a reminder of our own vulnerability and the precariousness of our taken-for-granted rights and freedoms. On television and in the movies the crime story gives us a chance to probe our own darker motives, to ask "Is there a criminal within?" as well as to feel the collective satisfaction of seeing justice done.

Fear and fascination, these two poles of our engagement with crime, are, of course, only part of the story. Crime is, after all, a major social and legal problem, not just an issue of our individual psychology. Politicians today use our fear of, and fascination with, crime for political advantage. How we respond to crime, as well as to the political uses of the crime issue, tells us a lot about who we are as a people as well as what we value and what we tolerate. Is our response compassionate or severe? Do we seek to understand or to punish, to enact an angry vengeance or to rehabilitate and welcome the criminal back into our midst? The CRIME, JUSTICE, AND PUNISHMENT series is designed to explore these themes, to ask why we are fearful and fascinated, to probe the meanings and motivations of crimes and criminals and of our responses to them, and, finally, to ask what we can learn about ourselves and the society in which we live by examining our responses to crime.

Crime is always a challenge to the prevailing normative order and a test of the values and commitments of law-abiding people. It is sometimes a Raskolnikov-like act of defiance, an assertion of the unwillingness of some to live according to the rules of conduct laid out by organized society. In this sense, crime marks the limits of the law and reminds us of law's all-too-regular failures. Yet sometimes there is more desperation than defiance in criminal acts; sometimes they signal a deep pathology or need in the criminal. To confront crime is thus also to come face-to-face with the reality of social difference, of class privilege and extreme deprivation, of race and racism, of children neglected, abandoned, or abused whose response is to enact on others what they have experienced themselves. And occasionally crime, or what is labeled a criminal act, represents a call for justice, an appeal to a higher moral order against the inadequacies of existing law.

Figuring out the meaning of crime and the motivations of criminals and whether crime arises from defiance, desperation, or the appeal for justice is never an easy task. The motivations and meanings of crime are as varied as are the persons who engage in criminal conduct. They are as mysterious as any of the mysteries of the human soul. Yet the desire to know the secrets of crime and the criminal is a strong one, for in that knowledge may lie one step on the road to protection, if not an assurance of one's own personal safety. Nonetheless, as strong as that desire may be, there is no available technology that can allow us to know the whys of crime with much confidence, let alone a scientific certainty. We can, however, capture something about crime by studying the defiance, desperation, and quest for justice that may be associated with it. Books in the Crime, Justice, and Punishment series will take up that challenge. They tell stories of crime and criminals, some famous, most not, some glamorous and exciting, most mundane and commonplace.

This series will, in addition, take a sober look at American criminal justice, at the procedures through which we investigate crimes and identify criminals, at the institutions in which innocence or guilt is determined. In these procedures and institutions we confront the thrill of the chase as well as the challenge of protecting the rights of those who defy our laws. It is through the efficiency and dedication of law enforcement that we might capture the criminal; it is in the rare instances of their corruption or brutality that we feel perhaps our deepest betrayal. Police, prosecutors, defense lawyers, judges, and jurors administer criminal justice and in their daily actions give substance to the guarantees of the Bill of Rights. What is an adversarial system of justice? How does it work? Why do we have it? Books in the Crime, Justice, and Punishment series will examine the thrill of the chase as we seek to capture the criminal. They will also reveal the drama and majesty of the criminal trial as well as the day-to-day reality of a criminal justice system in which trials are the exception and negotiated pleas of guilty are the rule.

When the trial is over or the plea has been entered, when we have separated the innocent from the guilty, the moment of punishment has arrived. The injunction to punish the guilty, to respond to pain inflicted by inflicting pain, is as old as civilization itself. "An eye for an eye and a tooth for a tooth" is a biblical reminder that punishment must measure pain for pain. But our response to the criminal must be better than and different from the crime itself. The biblical admonition, along with the constitutional prohibition of "cruel and unusual punishment," signals that we seek to punish justly and to be just not only in the determination of who can and should be punished, but in how we punish as well. But neither reminder tells us what to do with the wrongdoer. Do we rape the rapist, or burn the home of the arsonist? Surely justice and decency say no. But, if not, then how can and should we punish? In a world in which punishment is neither identical to the crime nor an automatic response to it, choices must be made and we must make them. Books in the CRIME, JUSTICE, AND PUNISHMENT series will examine those choices and the practices, and politics, of punishment. How do we punish and why do we punish as we do? What can we learn about the rationality and appropriateness of today's responses to crime by examining our past and its responses? What works? Is there, and can there be, a just measure of pain?

CRIME, JUSTICE, AND PUNISHMENT brings together books on some of the great themes of human social life. The books in this series capture our fear and fascination with crime and examine our responses to it. They remind us of the deadly seriousness of these subjects. They bring together themes in law, literature, and popular culture to challenge us to think again, to think anew, about subjects that go to the heart of who we are and how we can and will live together.

*   *   *   *   *

It is a sad fact of American life that race has played, and continues to play, such an important role in the criminal justice system, but it is a fact nonetheless. No one can think intelligently about issues of crime and punishment without confronting that fact. Delores Jones-Brown does exactly that. Through a careful examination of our history and a close-up study of the contemporary situation, she gives us a striking, and often upsetting, glimpse of American justice in black and white. She shows that the impact of race is pervasive, that African Americans live under suspicion and that legal officials routinely treat them in ways that are offensive at best and degrading at worst. If clearheaded thinking about social and political problems is an essential step along the way toward effective responses to those problems, this book will help all who read it begin that journey.

AMERICAN JUSTICE: A STUDY IN BLACK AND WHITE

"In the matter of the people of the state of California versus Orenthal James Simpson, we the jury find the defendant Orenthal James Simpson . . ."

When the forewoman of a jury in Los Angeles rose to speak these words on October 2, 1995, millions of Americans were watching. The nine-month-long criminal trial of O. J. Simpson—which had been called "the trial of the century"—was about to come to an end. As later events would bear out, however, the controversy surrounding the case would not soon disappear.

Simpson, an African-American actor, television personality, and former pro football star, had been accused of stabbing to death two people—his ex-wife, Nicole Brown Simpson, and her friend Ronald

---

Flanked by his attorneys, O. J. Simpson reacts to the verdict in his criminal trial for the murder of his ex-wife, Nicole Brown Simpson, and her friend Ron Goldman. The "trial of the century" had turned on race.

13

Goldman. Both victims were white.

Press coverage of the case had verged on the obsessive, and many Americans had followed the trial closely. Nearly everyone, it seemed, had an opinion about the defendant's guilt or innocence. Significantly, there was a strong correlation between the race of the observer and whether he or she thought Simpson was guilty. A frequently cited poll found that 70 percent of white Americans believed that Simpson had committed the murders, whereas 70 percent of black Americans believed that he had not.

In part, the reason people could rationally hold either view was that there were no known witnesses to the killings and the murder weapon was never recovered. The prosecution's case was purely circumstantial. It hinged on police investigative efforts and the analysis of forensic evidence.

Nevertheless, prosecutors thought they had a solid case. Anchoring that case was blood found at the crime scene (the home of Nicole Brown Simpson), in O. J. Simpson's Ford Bronco, and at his estate. Using DNA testing—a scientific technique that produces a genetic "fingerprint" from a sample of biological material such as blood, semen, skin, or bone—investigators determined that blood collected at the crime scene belonged to Simpson, as did drops of blood in his Ford Bronco and on his walkway. (DNA experts for the prosecution testified that the odds these blood samples came from someone other than the defendant were billions to one.) The blood of the victims also turned up, DNA tests revealed, in the Bronco, and a sock found in Simpson's bedroom contained 19 drops of his ex-wife's blood. At the crime scene police also recovered a knit hat that, forensic tests showed, contained both Simpson's hair and carpet fibers from his car. In addition, police found a pair of blood-soaked gloves—one at the murder scene and one on Simpson's property.

Simpson's attorneys, on the other hand, attacked

the reliability of the prosecution's evidence, in particular the DNA evidence. They focused on the slipshod way the blood samples had been collected and handled and pointed to the possibility that the samples had been contaminated by sloppy procedures at the crime labs where they were tested.

But the defense lawyers also suggested that the police had deliberately framed Simpson. Simpson's lawyers destroyed the credibility of one key prosecution witness, Los Angeles Police Department detective Mark Fuhrman, who had climbed over the gate of Simpson's estate on the night of the murders and found the bloody glove there. On the witness stand Fuhrman, a white man, had denied ever using the racial epithet *nigger*. But a screenwriter with whom he had worked testified that that was false—and she had tapes of their conversations to prove it. The implication was that Fuhrman was a racist and that he had taken the bloody glove from the crime scene and planted it at Simpson's estate. Simpson's attorneys also called into question the conduct of another white police detective, Philip Vannatter. In violation of proper procedure, Vannatter had failed to immediately turn over to the police lab a vial of blood drawn from O. J. Simpson for testing. Could he have sprinkled Simpson's blood at the crime scene? Could he, with Fuhrman and other police officers, have been part of a conspiracy to frame Simpson? The defense team tried to convince the jury that it was possible.

When the forewoman finished reading the Simpson verdict—". . . not guilty of the charge of murder"—the reaction among Americans was immediate and unusually emotional. And once again it was split largely along racial lines. For the most part, whites expressed shock, outrage, and horror. Blacks, on the other hand, reported feeling a mix of surprise, relief, even elation.

Why such a markedly different reaction? Perhaps the answer has to do with the vastly different experiences

The public reaction to the Simpson trials was unusually emotional—and largely divided along racial lines. Above: A mostly white crowd jeers the defendant as he leaves court. Opposite page: African-American supporters celebrate Simpson's acquittal.

that whites and blacks have had with law enforcement and the criminal justice system. In general, whites tend to trust the police—the majority of whom are also white—and are unlikely to have personally experienced law enforcement as anything but race-neutral. Clearly, most whites accepted at face value the evidence arrayed against O. J. Simpson and rejected the notion that the police had tried to frame him. Many blacks, on the other hand, didn't find the possibility of a police frame-up too far-fetched. But blacks are much more likely than whites to be singled out for police attention, and in various instances—including another famous case in Los Angeles, the 1991 beating of an unarmed black motorist by three white police officers—an element of racism has seemed to be at work. For appalled whites, though, the most important fact about the Simpson

verdict was that, as they saw it, a guilty man had gotten away with a brutal double murder. For many African Americans, however, the idea that someone might get away with murder wasn't quite as shocking. Two centuries of cases involving white killers and black victims had taught that lesson (see box, pages 18–19). Often, as blacks are painfully aware, justice in America has not been color-blind.

Somewhat lost in the roiling controversy was the fact that the Simpson acquittal could be explained on the actual merits of the case, without resorting to race. First of all, purely circumstantial cases are always difficult for prosecutors to win; jurors want to hear from an eyewitness or see a murder weapon with the defendant's fingerprints on it. Second, the prosecution in the Simpson trial made crucial blunders. For example, prosecutor Christopher Darden violated a basic rule of trial lawyering—never ask a question to which you don't already know the answer—when he had Simpson try on the murderer's bloodstained gloves in the courtroom. They appeared not to fit, and although that may have been due to shrinkage of the leather caused by the

Justice Denied, Justice Delayed

On August 20, 1955, two black youths, 14-year-old Emmett Till and his 17-year-old cousin Curtis Jones, boarded a train in Chicago and headed south to visit relatives in Money, Mississippi. During their visit, Emmett and Curtis went into town to buy some candy at Bryant's Grocery and Meat Market. Outside the store they met up with some local youths and started swapping stories. One of the locals dared Emmett to speak to Carolyn Bryant, the white woman who ran the store. Emmett went inside, bought some candy, and said "Bye, baby" to her as he left. The boys scrambled and ran out of town.

Several days later came a knock on the door: Emmett was abducted at gunpoint. Four days later his body, with a 75-pound cotton gin fan tied around his neck with barbed wire, was found at the bottom of the Tallahatchie River. The boy had been stripped naked and beaten, one eye had been gouged

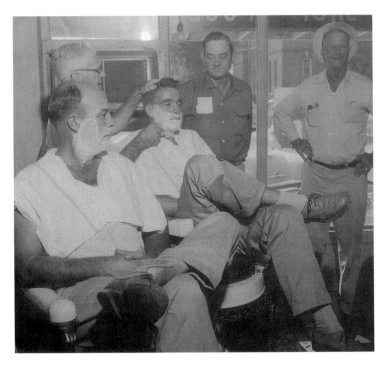

J. W. Milam (left) and Roy Bryant get a shave on the day of their arraignment for the kidnapping and murder of Emmett Till, a 14-year-old black youth. An all-white jury would acquit the two men after their lawyer appealed to the jurors' "Anglo-Saxon" sensibilities.

blood or the analysis of the blood, what the jurors saw was a dramatic demonstration that could only have raised doubts about the evidence. Third, exposing a hidden interest or bias on the part of a witness is always a legitimate means of impeaching the witness's credibility, and once Fuhrman had been shown to have lied

out, and he had been shot through the head with a .45 caliber automatic. Emmett's mutilated body could be identified only by a ring on his finger.

The white woman's husband, Roy Bryant, and his brother-in-law J. W. Milam were arrested and charged with kidnapping and murder. Initially they admitted abducting Emmett but denied killing him. The two men went on trial in a segregated courthouse in Sumner, Mississippi, on September 19, 1955. Emmett's 64-year-old great-uncle, Mose Wright, identified the two defendants as the men who had abducted his nephew. After his testimony, he and other blacks who testified against the two had to be hurried out of the state for their safety.

Defense attorney John C. Whitten told the white jurors, "Your fathers will turn over in their graves if [Milam and Bryant are found guilty] and I'm sure that every last Anglo-Saxon one of you has the courage to free these men." The jury deliberated for a little over an hour and returned a not guilty verdict. One juror later remarked that they would have been done even quicker had they not stopped to drink a soda pop.

•   •   •

Twenty minutes past midnight on June 12, 1963, Medgar Evers pulled his family Oldsmobile into the carport of his house. After a long day of work, the 37-year-old field secretary for the National Association for the Advancement of Colored People (NAACP) was awaited by his wife and three children. Carrying paperwork and sweatshirts that read Jim Crow Must Go, he stepped into the light of the carport, unaware that Ku Klux Klansman Byron de la Beckwith was hiding in the bushes of a vacant lot across the street. Beckwith aimed his rifle and fired. Fifteen minutes after arriving at the University of Mississippi Hospital, Evers was pronounced dead.

Beckwith dropped the murder weapon at the scene, and it had his fingerprints on it. He had earlier spoken of his desire to kill Evers and after the murder was even said to have bragged that he was the killer. Yet at two trials in 1964, the all-white, male juries deadlocked, and Beckwith remained a free man.

In 1989, however, evidence surfaced of jury tampering in the earlier trials, and the district attorney filed new charges against Beckwith. He was rearrested in 1990. In 1994, more than 30 years after the crime, Beckwith was finally found guilty of murdering Medgar Evers. The third jury was composed of six men and six women, eight of whom were black.

under oath about a racial matter, jurors were more likely to doubt the rest of his testimony. Nor is attacking police procedures a tactic pioneered by Simpson's attorneys, and by all accounts much of the police work in the Simpson investigation was sloppy. Finally, American criminal procedure requires that to convict, a jury must have proof "beyond a reasonable doubt" of the defendant's guilt. Simpson's acquittal may merely have reflected the jurors' views that reasonable doubt about his guilt existed.

Despite the plausible legal explanations for the not guilty verdict, many Americans—legal experts and laypeople alike—focused on the issue of race, thereby exposing and aggravating bitter divisions between black and white America. Many whites, including members of the news media, complained that Simpson's lawyers had deliberately injected race into the trial to save what would have been a losing case. Many painted the acquittal as the "wrong" verdict made by an incompetent, overly emotional, and—not coincidentally—mostly black jury. For many African Americans, such suggestions sounded a discordant and ironic note. The kind of outrage whites felt at the Simpson verdict seemed curiously absent in cases when white defendants were acquitted of crimes against blacks. Many blacks agreed that race was at the heart of the Simpson matter, but not quite the way whites thought. The case, declared Dennis Schatzman, a journalism professor and columnist for black newspapers, "was about the criminal law system and how it treats black people. And O. J. Simpson had the resources to fight an obviously racist and biased system and he prevailed playing by their rules."

But Simpson would not prevail in the next legal contest, a civil suit brought by the families of Ronald Goldman and Nicole Brown Simpson and decided in January 1997. This time, a mostly white jury found Simpson liable (responsible) for the wrongful deaths of the victims and ordered him to pay $33.5 million in compensatory and punitive damages. Once again, the verdict could have been explained on legal grounds alone. Most significantly, the standard of proof in a civil trial is only "a preponderance of the evidence," which might be translated as "more likely than not"— a much lower standard than the criminal trial's "proof beyond a reasonable doubt." Yet once again, much of the public reaction and media coverage seemed to focus on race. Analysts noted that the jury in the civil trial was primarily white, whereas the jury in the criminal case had been predominantly black. Whites were depicted as celebrating the civil verdict, which, they thought, allowed justice to be served. Blacks, on the other hand, were portrayed as angry protesters. Whites characterized the civil verdict as the "right" decision made by a competent jury; some blacks suggested that the whole procedure had been designed merely to "get" the defendant.

What do the Simpson trials say about American justice? One disturbing though plausible answer is that the legal process will always be shadowed by issues of race. Some social science research suggests, for example, that it may have been easier for white people to see Simpson as a criminal simply because he is a black man, despite defense efforts to discredit the evidence against him. Other research suggests that it may have been more natural for blacks, including the jurors, to distrust the validity of the evidence because most of it was gathered by police.

Whether or not these specific factors were actually present in the disposition of the Simpson cases, the long history of race and racism in America has shaped the perceptions of both black and white citizens, particularly with regard to crime and punishment. The image of justice as a blind lady may be a reassuring, but ultimately delusive, symbol. It appears that where race is involved, even the law cannot be neutral.

2.

A DOUBLE STANDARD: RACE, CRIME, AND LAW IN AMERICAN HISTORY

Many people believe that the connection between race and crime in America, which the Simpson verdicts once again brought to the forefront of public consciousness, is a phenomenon of recent origin. Many people also believe that the connection is accidental. Neither belief is correct. In fact, race and crime have been linked since the earliest days of British colonization in America. And, far from being accidental, the link was created and has been reinforced by hundreds of years of law.

Around 1619 the first African slaves were imported to the American colonies. Obviously, a society that places high value on liberty will have a difficult time justifying holding a group of people in bondage. The solution, of course, was to deny the humanity of the slaves; in the eyes of society they were merely property. And this special status required special treatment under the law.

In the late 1600s the southern colonies began

Colonists examine a shipment of African slaves at Jamestown, Virginia, 1619. The tangled history of race, crime, and punishment in America began in the 17th century, with the enactment of laws designed to control the slave population.

The Constitution of the United States never uses the word slavery. *But America's Founding Fathers provided the legal framework that allowed the continuation of that institution, even going so far as to specify that each slave should be counted as three-fifths of a person.*

enacting Slave Codes. These codes, designed for the discipline and control of a subject population, established a dual legal system—one set of laws for whites and another for their black slaves. The codes essentially gave masters complete authority to treat their slaves as they saw fit, providing for punishment in the form of whipping, branding, castration, or brutal methods of execution. Slave owners could even beat a slave to death without being prosecuted. But the Slave Codes also prohibited the granting of certain rights or privileges to slaves: by law slaves could not carry weapons, own property, or have any legal rights or protections. This, of course, further set them apart from whites.

In 1776, in the midst of the Revolutionary War, America's leaders presented a high-minded case for breaking away from England in the Declaration of Independence. "We hold these truths to be self-evident," they stated, "that all men are created equal, that they are endowed by their Creator with certain unalienable Rights, that among these are Life, Liberty, and the pursuit of Happiness." What was not self-evident to the signers of the Declaration of Independence was that their African slaves might be endowed with certain unalienable rights as well. While the signers denounced the tyranny of King George III, they were silent on the issue of slavery.

In 1787, after the success of the Revolutionary War and a brief, failed experiment at a loose confederation of states, some of America's most influential political leaders gathered in Philadelphia to draft a federal constitution. Several delegates from northern states argued that the institution of slavery should be abolished, but their colleagues from the South adamantly disagreed, and the controversy threatened to break up the Constitutional Convention.

In the end the delegates largely skirted the issue. The U.S. Constitution never uses the terms *slave* or *slavery*. But in deliberately vague language, the Constitution's authors did provide the legal framework for the continuation of slavery in America. Article 1, Section 2 specified that, for the apportionment of U.S. representatives and of direct taxes, the states' populations "be determined by adding to the whole Number of free Persons . . . three fifths of all other Persons." (Slaves, the "other Persons," were thus to be counted as 60 percent of a white human being.) Section 9 of the same article forbade Congress from prohibiting, until 1808, "the Migration or Importation of such Persons as any of the States now existing shall think proper to admit." And Article 4, Section 2 required that any "Person held to Service or Labour in one State, under the Laws thereof" who escaped to another state "be delivered up on Claim [of] the Party to whom such Service or Labour may be due," regardless of the laws in the state to which the slave had escaped. So while the preamble to the Constitution listed among its primary goals to "establish Justice . . . and secure the Blessings of Liberty to ourselves and our Posterity [descendants]," the same document tacitly acknowledged that the meaning of justice varied across race and circumstance, and it expressly prohibited black slaves from pursuing the blessings of liberty. The Constitution left intact the old Slave Codes, and runaway slaves thus became the first large group of criminals in the United States.

But being a runaway or disobedient slave wasn't the only "offense" the Slave Codes criminalized. Nor were slaves the only group the codes punished. In a sense, America's dual legal system criminalized blackness itself, for while the laws may have been designed to uphold the institution of slavery, they singled out all people of African descent, including free black residents, for different treatment.

In *Criminalizing a Race: Free Blacks During Slavery*, former Rutgers University professor Charsee McIntyre documents the numerous laws and legal practices that, for free African Americans, created crimes out of liberties guaranteed to others. Free blacks had resided in the American colonies since the first days of slave importation. And although they weren't considered more criminal than any other immigrant ethnic group, various statutes restricted their freedom to live where they chose as well as their freedom of movement. As early as 1691, for example, Virginia and North Carolina had maintained statutes making it unlawful for free blacks to reside there. In Connecticut, under the terms of a law in effect from 1774 to 1797, all blacks had to have a written pass to travel outside their hometown; violators were fined. Later the state of Maryland imposed a $50 fine against free blacks who entered the state and an additional $50 per week for remaining. In jurisdictions with similar restrictions, free blacks who could not pay such fines were arrested and enslaved. Even the non–slave state of Ohio prohibited blacks, as late as 1804, from becoming permanent residents unless they could furnish a "certificate of freedom" issued by some court of the United States.

In addition to restricting where blacks could live, various laws also limited the jobs they could hold. For example, a South Carolina statute that took effect in 1834 made it a crime for a black person to work as a store clerk or salesman. The law also authorized punishment for any white person who would hire a black for such a position:

> If any person shall employ or keep as a clerk, any person of color, or shall permit any slave or free person of color to act as a clerk or salesman, in or about any shop, store or house used for trading, such person shall be liable to be indicted therefor and upon conviction thereof, shall be fined for each and every offense not exceeding one hundred dollars, and be imprisoned not exceeding six months; the informer to be a competent witness, and to be entitled to one half of the fine.

Various southern jurisdictions also criminalized education for blacks. A typical statute, from South Carolina in 1835, prohibited anyone from teaching any person of color—slave or free—to read or write. Whites who violated this law were subject to a fine of up to $100 and six months' imprisonment. Free blacks could receive up to 50 lashes with a whip and a $50 fine, and slaves could receive 50 lashes.

Although the worst abuses occurred in the South, blacks weren't treated equally in the North either. Massachusetts and Rhode Island, for example, had an economic interest in slavery because large numbers of slave shipments passed through their ports. New York, New Jersey, and Massachusetts maintained segregation in schools, social clubs, and the trades. And, as archaeologists recently discovered, in New York blacks and whites weren't even equal in death: segregated burial places existed.

Nor can the responsibility of the federal government

be overlooked in maintaining a legal system that subordinated blacks to all other Americans. In addition to the fugitive slave clause within the Constitution (Article 4, Section 2), two separate federal statutes were enacted—one in 1793 and an amended version in 1850—that mandated the return of runaway slaves. These laws imposed a legal obligation on all Americans, whether pro-slavery or abolitionist, to report all runaway slaves and otherwise assist in their capture. Failure to do so could lead to federal prosecution resulting in fines and imprisonment. The Fugitive Slave Act of 1850 also authorized slave owners ("their attorneys or assigns") to recruit, for the purpose of assisting in the recovery of their "property," officers in the so-called slave patrol. In reality, many of these officers were untrained citizens, and their methods tended to be quite ruthless. The statute even "authorized and required" payment to those assisting in the capture and transport of the "criminals."

Like the federal government, the courts also bore significant responsibility for perpetuating America's dual legal system. In the 1850s the United States Supreme Court had the opportunity to expand the circumstances under which black slaves might gain their liberty and thus bring legal reality more in line with the lofty promises in the Declaration of Independence and the Constitution. Instead the Court's ruling dramatically restricted the legal status of all blacks. The case, which the Court heard in 1856, was *Dred Scott v. Sandford*.

Dred Scott was a slave whose master, John Emerson, was a surgeon in the U.S. Army. Emerson took Scott to his successive posts in the slave state of Missouri, the free state of Illinois, and the free territory of Minnesota. After Emerson was reassigned to Missouri, he died. Scott tried unsuccessfully to buy his freedom from Emerson's widow, then sued in court. He claimed that he should be free because of his long stays in Illinois and

When Dred Scott, a slave, sued for his freedom, the U.S. Supreme Court ruled that no one of "the negro race"—slave or free—could be an American citizen in the sense in which the Constitution used the word.

Minnesota, which were free soil. Mrs. Emerson's lawyers countered that once he stepped back onto Missouri soil, he became subject to Missouri law. While his case proceeded in the lower courts, Scott became the property of Mrs. Emerson's brother, John Sanford.

Scott eventually sued Sanford, in federal court, for assault. The suit hinged on Scott's claim to be a citizen, because a slaveholder couldn't be charged with mistreating his "property." Eventually the case found its way to the U.S. Supreme Court.

On March 6, 1857, the Court delivered its ruling in *Dred Scott v. Sandford* (John Sanford's name had been misspelled). In a 7-2 decision, the justices found against Dred Scott. The Court ruled that "the right of property in a slave is distinctly and expressly affirmed in the Constitution." But the ruling went much further, denying that any black could be an American citizen "in the sense in which the word citizen is used in the Constitution of the United States." The Constitution's framers, Chief Justice Roger B. Taney wrote, understood blacks to be "a subordinate and inferior class of beings" and never intended to include them within the meaning of the phrase "We the People of the United States." Thus the law of the land, as interpreted by America's highest court, held that no one of "the negro race," whether slave or free, was entitled to "the rights and privileges conferred by the Constitution upon citizens." The Declaration of Independence may have elevated liberty to the status of an "unalienable right," but that right applied to whites only.

Scholars point to the Dred Scott case as one of many factors that pushed the United States toward the Civil War, which broke out four years after the Supreme Court's ruling. In the wake of the North's victory in 1865 came the enactment of the Thirteenth Amendment, which abolished slavery in the United States. In the short term, however, this did little to improve the legal status of African Americans in the South.

Between 1865 and 1866, many southern states enacted Black Codes. These laws restricted the rights and behavior of newly freed African Americans in much the same manner as had the old Slave Codes. The Black Codes, for example, limited the rights of African Americans to own or rent property; forbade them from bearing arms or meeting in unsupervised groups; allowed blacks to be imprisoned for breach of employment contracts (whites were subject only to fines); and denied blacks the right to bring charges or testify against whites in court (except when testifying about violations of the codes themselves).

So complete was the control of African Americans under the Black Codes that in many towns they could legally work only at menial jobs and were forbidden from being on the streets after dark.

In response to abuses such as these, Congress drafted the Fourteenth and Fifteenth Amendments, which were quickly ratified. The Fourteenth Amendment made everyone born or naturalized in the United States a citizen of both the United States and the state in which he or she resided. Furthermore, it prohibited any state from abridging the "privileges or immunities" of American citizens. In other words, if a citizen had a legal right in one part of the United States, no state could take away that right. Finally, the amendment said that no state could "deny to any person within its jurisdiction the equal protection of the laws." The Fifteenth Amendment said that no citizen could be denied the right to vote "on account of race, color, or previous condition of servitude."

With the ratification of these amendments and the passage of the Civil Rights Act of 1866, which was designed to guarantee the rights of freed slaves, blacks had at last theoretically achieved equality under the law. In fact, nearly a century would pass before America would approach legal equality for its black and white citizens.

The primary reason for continued legalized inequality were the Jim Crow laws, which the southern states enacted, and the Supreme Court upheld, in the last two decades of the 19th century. These laws essentially circumvented the intent of the Fourteenth and Fifteenth Amendments.

Named for a black character (played by a white entertainer in blackface) in an old minstrel show song-and-dance routine, Jim Crow laws served to keep black and white societies separate. They mandated separate facilities for nearly every facet of public life in the South—schools, dining areas, transportation, bathrooms. Legal segregation of the races, southern legislators argued, wasn't the same as inequality under the law.

In 1896 the Supreme Court had the chance to decide the constitutionality of Jim Crow in the landmark case of *Plessy v. Ferguson*. Homer Plessy, a 30-year-old shoemaker from New Orleans, had been arrested on June 7, 1892, for sitting in a car reserved for white passengers of the East Louisiana railroad. He was charged with criminally violating an 1890 ordinance separating railway car passengers by race. Ironically, Plessy was seven-eighths white and one-eighth African American, but the prevailing legal definition of the period was that "one drop" of African blood made a person "Negro" or "colored."

Plessy's bail was set at $500 and he was later convicted. He appealed to the Supreme Court, arguing that the Louisiana statute violated the Thirteenth and Fourteenth Amendments and that mandatory segregation could only stamp blacks with a "badge of inferiority." The Supreme Court disagreed. In an 8-1 decision, the justices upheld the Louisiana statute and Plessy's conviction.

Writing for the majority, Justice Henry B. Brown denied that the statute violated the Thirteenth or Fourteenth Amendments and noted:

> A statute which implies merely a legal distinction between the white and colored races—a distinction which is founded in the color of the two races and which must always exist so long as white men are distinguished from the other race by color—has no tendency to destroy the legal equality of the two races. . . .
>
> We consider the underlying fallacy of the plaintiff's argument to consist in the assumption that the enforced separation of the two races stamps the colored race with a badge of inferiority. If this be so, it is not by reason of anything found in the act, but solely because the colored race chooses to put that construction upon it.

In hindsight, Brown and the Court could not have

been more wrong. Only Justice John Harlan, the sole dissenter in the *Plessy* decision, foresaw the harm that would be created by the Court's ruling. In disagreeing with his fellow justices, he warned:

> Our Constitution is color-blind, and neither knows nor tolerates classes among citizens. In respect of civil rights, all citizens are equal before the law. . . . In my opinion, the judgment this day rendered will, in time prove to be quite as pernicious as the decision made by this tribunal in the *Dred Scott* case. . . . The present decision, it may well be apprehended, will not only stimulate aggressions, more or less brutal and irritating, upon the admitted rights of colored citizens, but will encourage the belief that it is possible, by means of state enactments, to co-opt recent amendments of the Constitution.

Justice Harlan's warnings notwithstanding, the Court upheld the constitutionality of official segregation, provided that the facilities for blacks and whites were equal. (Of course, the facilities inevitably *weren't* equal, but the "separate but equal" doctrine stood unchallenged until the Supreme Court's 1954 decision in the case of *Brown v. Board of Education of Topeka*, which outlawed segregation in the public schools.)

Official, legally sanctioned inequality was only one aspect of blacks' unequal treatment, however. Law enforcement and prosecution often took very different forms depending on the race of the victim and of the perpetrator. And unofficial methods of "justice," such as lynching, were frequently used to terrorize entire black communities and to punish individual blacks accused of offenses ranging from murder or the rape of a white woman to insulting a white person or simply startling a white child.

Lynchings, which might occur during the cover of night or in broad daylight, customarily included abducting a victim, then hanging, dragging through the streets, shooting, or burning him—or her. Lynchings became so commonplace—more than 5,000 have been

Justice John Marshall Harlan, the lone dissenter in the case of Plessy v. Ferguson, *warned that the Supreme Court's 1896 decision would "stimulate aggressions, more or less brutal and irritating, upon the admitted rights of colored citizens." He was right, as the* Plessy *case paved the way for the Jim Crow laws that would remain in effect until the civil rights movement of the mid-20th century.*

A lynching in Boyston, Georgia, 1936. Equality under the law meant little when whites could lynch African Americans with impunity.

documented between 1859 and 1918—that they were sometimes advertised in newspapers, providing a perverse spectator sport. These public lynching events were particularly brutal. Lynch mobs consisted primarily of white men, although women and children were often present as spectators and male children were sometimes permitted to participate. African-American men were most often the victims, though Hispanics, Native Americans, and black women and children were sometimes lynched as well. Following a lynching, body parts (particularly ears and fingers of the victim) might be taken or distributed (even sold) as souvenirs. Sometimes, after completing their deadly work, lynch mobs would ride through the black section of town, assaulting random black victims and burning black-owned homes and businesses. Most lynchings—especially those that were accompanied by destruction of black neighborhoods—occurred in the South, but such communities as Chicago; Tulsa, Oklahoma; and East St. Louis, Missouri; were also severely affected.

Lynching, it must be emphasized, was completely incompatible with norms of justice. It punished whatever behavior the mob objected to, even when that behavior didn't constitute a crime (or in many cases, even when the alleged offense hadn't even occurred). Lynching also made a mockery of the rights and procedural protections all people accused of a crime in the United States are supposed to receive; the lynch mob functioned as judge, jury, and executioner. Ultimately, lynching was murder, plain and simple.

Yet it was rarely punished. In part, this was because police and the court systems, especially in the South, turned a blind eye and sometimes even cooperated in lynch mobs' work. And in the rare instances when lynch mob participants were actually prosecuted, convictions were almost never obtained. The reasons: in

Scenes from a Lynching, as Reported by the New York *Herald*, June 9, 1903

The crowd in the jail broke into Wyatt's cell. He fought fiercely for his life, but a blow from a sledge hammer felled him. A rope was tied around his neck. He was dragged out into the corridor, down the stairs and into the jail yard, then into Spring Street, up to Main Street and to the center of the square.

A man riding a white horse led the way to an electric light pole in the square. The end of the rope was thrown over it, and the body was drawn up above the heads of the crowd, who cheered and waved hats. Men on the pole kicked Wyatt in the face. The swaying form was stabbed repeatedly. Mutilations followed.

Kerosene was bought and poured over the body and it was set on fire, while the crowd cheered. The rope burned through and the body fell. More kerosene was poured on the body as the flames slowly consumed it.

some areas blacks were prohibited from testifying against whites, whites wouldn't testify on behalf of blacks, and a white judge and an all-white jury sympathetic to the defendant typically heard such cases. (Though in 1880 the Supreme Court overturned laws explicitly prohibiting blacks from serving on juries, African-American jurors were routinely excluded by judges and lawyers anyway.) John Whitten, the lawyer for the men accused of murdering black teenager Emmett Till in Money, Mississippi, was thus able to appeal to the jury's "Anglo-Saxon" sensibilities (see box, p. 18–19).

White judges and all-white juries gave whites accused of crimes against blacks an enormous legal advantage, but they also ensured that most blacks tried for crimes against whites would not fare well. In the South particularly, black defendants didn't stand much of a chance, especially when they were accused of violent offenses against whites. The alleged rape of a white woman in the South, many black men found out, meant an almost automatic death sentence—that is, if the defendant was fortunate enough to avoid being lynched before his trial. Often, the actual evidence upon which the prosecution rested didn't matter.

A famous, though probably not atypical, miscarriage of justice occurred in Alabama in 1931, when nine black youths ranging in age from 13 to 21, who came to be known as the Scottsboro Boys, were tried for the alleged rape of two young white women on a freight train. (The women, who were unmarried, had apparently concocted the story to cover up the fact that they had had sex with two white men and to avoid possible jail sentences for vagrancy.) According to the women's testimony, the black youths had held them at knifepoint and all nine defendants had participated in the rapes; each woman said she was raped six times. But the evidence simply didn't add up. When they got off the train, both women were fully dressed and showed

no signs of a struggle. And doctors who examined them found no signs of forced intercourse, which would have been inevitable had each woman been forcibly raped six times. Nevertheless, the trial, which took a mere three days, ended in the conviction of all nine defendants. With the exception of the youngest, all were sentenced to die in the electric chair.

The case drew a huge amount of publicity, however, and attorneys from the International Labor Defense (ILD), an arm of the Communist Party, filed appeals for the Scottsboro Boys. Eventually the Supreme Court ordered new trials. By March 1933, when defendant Haywood Patterson's retrial began, Ruby Bates, one of the two women who had brought the original accusa-

Eight of the nine Scottsboro Boys, who were convicted of gang-raping two white women in Alabama despite abundant evidence that no rapes had occurred.

tions, had recanted her story. On the witness stand Bates admitted that she and her companion, Victoria Price, had made everything up; no rapes had ever occurred. Still, this jury, once again composed entirely of whites, voted to convict. Although the judge threw out the verdict, Patterson was again convicted at a third trial. The other Scottsboro defendants also were convicted.

In 1935, however, the Supreme Court once again overturned the convictions, this time because the counties where the Scottsboro Boys' trials had been held prohibited blacks from serving on grand juries. Though by this time it was clear to everyone—including the editors of the South's major newspapers—that the Scottsboro Boys were innocent, the prosecutor again filed charges against the five oldest. (The others received pardons in 1937.) And once again, the retrials ended in convictions for all the defendants, who received prison sentences ranging from 20 to 99 years. Haywood Patterson, the last Scottsboro defendant to gain his freedom, finally escaped from prison in 1948 after spending 17 years behind bars.

*   *   *

Some Americans would argue that events such as the Scottsboro Boys' trials of the 1930s or the murder of Emmett Till in the 1950s—like the Slave Codes and the Black Codes and the thousands of lynchings that went before—have little or no bearing on issues of race, crime, and punishment at the dawn of the 21st century. Deplorable and shameful though they were, they nonetheless represent only painful reminders of a distant and receding past, finished chapters in America's progress toward greater justice for all.

Such a belief may be overly optimistic. Is it likely that a legal system that for hundreds of years created crimes for one group out of liberties granted to another would leave no legacy? Is it possible that a system that for so long could not, or would not, protect one group from violence committed by another could easily be forgotten? Could centuries of a double standard of justice really produce no lingering injustice?

For many blacks living in the United States today, recent instances of apparent bias in law enforcement and criminal justice only reinforce lessons taught over and over by America's long history of inequality under the law: being black in America means being more vulnerable. The police are not impartial, and if blackness is no longer criminalized outright, it remains a factor in harsher treatment by the criminal justice system.

For white America, the legacy of official racism may be equally profound. The legal scholars Rollin M. Perkins and Ronald N. Boyce have asserted that "an incidental but very important function of the criminal law is to teach the difference between right and wrong." If this is so, what lessons might whites have learned—perhaps even unconsciously—from America's long history of criminalizing black conduct and denying African Americans equal rights under the law? Perhaps that blacks are more criminal as a group and that they don't deserve the same rights, protections, and privileges as whites. Unfortunately, this attitude has not disappeared; rather, it has been fueled by such factors as the dubious use of crime statistics and exaggerated fears of interracial victimization. America's troubled racial past endures in the fears and misperceptions of the present.

3.

RACE AND CRIME: FEARS AND FACTS

"A crime quiz: Which candidate gave weekend passes to rapists and murderers who weren't even eligible for parole?" The voice-over asked this question while on-screen was the photograph of a black man. The political ad went on to give its answer: "Michael Dukakis."

Dukakis, the governor of Massachusetts, was the Democratic Party's nominee for president in 1988, when the television commercial for his Republican opponent, George Bush, aired. Clearly, the commercial was intended to paint Dukakis as "soft on crime" and to play on a fear felt by many Americans: the fear of becoming a crime victim. The black man depicted in the political ad, Willie Horton, had been released from a Massachusetts prison on a weekend furlough and had fled to Maryland, where he raped a white woman.

Another Bush campaign commercial hammered away at the same Dukakis-is-soft-on-crime theme. "His revolving-door prison policy," the voice-over declared,

Black offender, white victim: how many Americans view patterns of crime. But statistics indicate that interracial crime such as the attempted robbery shown here is relatively rare.

The face that turned an election? Political ads depicting Willie Horton, the convicted murderer who raped a white woman after escaping from a Massachusetts prison during a furlough, may have been the decisive factor in the 1988 presidential race.

"gave weekend furloughs to first-degree murderers not eligible for parole." The image, filmed in black and white, showed a seemingly endless line of convicts moving in slow motion through a revolving door of prison bars. "Now Michael Dukakis says he wants to do for America what he's done for Massachusetts," the announcer continued. "America can't afford that risk."

In the November election, America apparently agreed. Bush handily defeated Dukakis to become the 41st president of the United States, and his television commercials were cited as a major factor in his victory.

The Bush campaign had successfully tapped into a long tradition in American politics—namely, exploiting the crime issue for political gain. But critics saw another, more sinister factor at work in the TV commercials: racism. Was it a coincidence, they wondered, that a black man had been selected to show that Michael Dukakis was soft on crime? There were, after all, white prisoners released under the Massachusetts furlough program who had escaped and committed crimes. Why hadn't one of them been pictured instead of Willie Horton? Was it also a coincidence that the crime Horton committed after his escape—the rape of a white woman—has elicited visceral fears and explosive reactions among whites since before the Civil War?

A close examination of the "revolving door" commercial added credibility to the critics' charges of deliberate racism. The convicts entering (prison) through the revolving door were white; the men exiting (to freedom) were black and Hispanic. The message, critics declared, was not simply that Dukakis released black criminals onto the streets. Writing in the *Columbia Journalism Review*, media scholar and Johns Hopkins University professor Mark Crispin Miller stated that the revolving door implied "that the Dukakis prison system was not only porous, but a satanic source of negritude—a dark 'liberal' mill that took white men and made them colored."

Of course, most Americans couldn't have articulated, in such a sophisticated manner, the subtle manipulation of images at work in the Bush commercials. Many viewers probably couldn't even have said why the commercials struck a nerve. The likeliest explanation, however, is race: consciously or unconsciously, many white Americans view black men as the "criminal element," and they especially fear being violently victimized by blacks. Author and political science professor Andrew Hacker demonstrates this in a hypothetical exercise with his students. He asks white students to choose between having $300 stolen from them by someone white, or having $100 stolen from them by someone black. Almost invariably the students select the first scenario. In other words, they are willing to lose an extra $200 just to avoid an encounter with a black assailant. It was this kind of white fear, critics charged, that the Bush media directors both exploited and reinforced.

Ironically, where crime in America is concerned, white fears are starkly at odds with the facts. Statistics show that whites commit a far-greater number of crimes than do blacks, and moreover, whites are not likely to be violently victimized by African Americans. Indeed, those who have the most to fear from black criminals are other blacks.

The statistical picture of crime in America comes largely from two sources: the Uniform Crime Reports (UCR), compiled annually by the Federal Bureau of Investigation from information collected from jurisdictions nationwide; and the National Crime Victimization Survey (NCVS), based on interviews with about 49,000 scientifically selected households, conducted by the Justice Department's Bureau of Justice Statistics.

The NCVS is designed to capture information about crimes that go unreported and thus don't show up in the UCR data.

According to UCR figures, a total of 11,072,832 arrests were recorded in 1996, the most recent year for which national statistics are available. Of those arrested, 7,404,170, or roughly two-thirds (66.9 percent), were white; just over 30 percent (3,400,338) were black; and the remaining 2.5 percent (roughly 250,000) were individuals of other racial or ethnic categories.

Besides recording the overall number of arrests, the UCR tracks crime by offense type, ranging from murder to motor vehicle theft to loitering. In addition, eight selected offenses in two categories—violent crime and property crime—make up what is called the Crime Index, an important tool for understanding and monitoring crime trends. The four offenses in the Crime Index's violent crime category are murder/nonnegligent

Race and Youth Crime: The Persistence of Images

In the minds of many people, the young black male has become the prototype of the American criminal. This perception exists despite the fact that in a typical year whites account for more than two-thirds of all juveniles (persons under age 18) arrested. However, many Americans' only exposure to serious crime is through the media, where depictions of violent and sociopathic black youths have become commonplace.

During the late 1980s and throughout the 1990s, movie theaters were flooded with films that purported to depict the realities of urban life in the United States. These movies, including *Boyz N the Hood*, *Juice*, *Menace II Society*, and *Set It Off*, were peopled with young African-American characters immersed in a world of violence and brutality. Though often deemed realistic and sometimes well received by the critics, such films no doubt increased fears of predatory black youths—especially among white viewers who had never ventured into an urban ghetto.

The music industry has also played a part in perpetuating the image of the young black male as criminal. Beginning in the early 1990s record companies aggressively marketed so-called gangsta rap, a form of rap music whose lyrics seemed to glorify violence and gang membership among blacks. For many Americans the murders of rappers Tupac Shakur and Notorious B.I.G. appeared only to confirm the existence of an ultraviolent black urban subculture.

manslaughter (criminal homicide), forcible rape, robbery, and aggravated assault. The index crimes against property are burglary, larceny-theft, motor vehicle theft, and arson. Obviously, when Americans worry about being the victim of crime, they are more concerned about violent crime than about property crime.

An examination of the Crime Index amplifies what the UCR's raw arrest figures indicate: despite perceptions to the contrary, African Americans do *not* commit the majority of violent crime. In 1996, for example, the number of white people arrested for violent crimes exceeded the number of black people arrested by more than 60,000—299,010 to 236,343.

However, figures for the individual index crimes do reveal that black arrests exceeded white arrests for the offenses of murder/nonnegligent manslaughter (7,928 versus 6,176) and robbery (70,828 versus 48,412). On the other hand, more whites than blacks were arrested for aggravated assault (230,785 versus 147,463) and forcible rape (13,637 versus 10,124).

The prevalent myth that whites are at a higher risk of being victimized by black criminals than by white criminals, which may help explain the effectiveness of the Willie Horton ad campaign, doesn't hold up under statistical analysis. For example, combined UCR and NCVS data indicate that forcible rape—the crime Horton committed after escaping during his furlough—is overwhelmingly an intraracial crime. In fully three-quarters of the cases, offenders and victims come from the same racial group.

The same holds true for criminal homicides. UCR figures from 1995 show that only 15 percent of white murder victims were killed by black offenders, and only 5 percent of black murder victims by white offenders. In raw numbers, this 10 percent difference in interracial killings amounts to roughly 957 deaths.

If the statistics dispel the myth of an epidemic of black-on-white violence, they do bear out a shocking reality: more blacks than whites are murder *victims*. In 1995, according to UCR figures, there were 9,694 black murder victims and 9,613 white murder victims. That is a difference of only 81 people, but in 1995 the black population in the United States was estimated at roughly 33 million, whereas the white population was approximately 218 million. Although they make up less than 13 percent of the total American population, African Americans suffer about half the murders.

This disproportionally high victimization rate holds for other categories of violent crime as well. Blacks are also more likely than whites or persons of other races to be victims of robbery or aggravated assault. Statistically, those who are the most vulnerable to violent victimization are the young, blacks, and males. Other characteristics that make individuals more vulnerable to violent victimization are being Hispanic and residing in an inner city. As a group, Hispanics have higher violent crime victimization rates than do non-Hispanics.

The chances of being the victim of sexual assault or rape don't vary significantly across race. NCVS data indicate that poverty is a better predictor than race of potential victimization: in 1994, persons in households with annual incomes of less than $15,000 were three times more likely to be raped or sexually assaulted than were persons in households with incomes greater than $15,000.

Income is a predictor of victimization rates for various property crimes as well. For example, households earning less than $7,500 a year suffered almost twice the rate of household burglary as did those earning up to $50,000, according to the 1994 NCVS. Renters also experienced significantly higher property crime rates compared with home owners, as did city residents compared with either suburban or rural residents. And, as with violent crime, black households experienced higher rates of property crime victimization than did white households (341 versus 302 incidents per

1,000 households). Hispanic households also had a considerably higher rate of victimization than did non-Hispanic households (426 versus 298 incidents per 1,000 households).

Overall, then, it appears that being poor, a minority (that is, African American or Hispanic), and an urban dweller increase the probability that an individual will be the victim of both violent and property crime. Not surprisingly, given continued patterns of segregated living in the United States, offenders tend to share these same characteristics with their victims—which is consistent with the observation that most crime is intraracial.

If analysis of crime statistics explodes the myth that whites have the most to fear from black criminals, it seems to confirm another popular belief: that blacks are disproportionally involved in crime, particularly violent crime. It must be reiterated that whites account for a far-greater *number* of crimes and that in nearly every offense category more whites than blacks are arrested. It also must be stressed that the vast majority of blacks, like the vast majority of whites, are law-abiding citizens. But the number of criminal offenses that blacks commit, the statistics indicate, is significantly out of proportion to their less than 13 percent representation in the U.S. population.

The 1996 statistics for forcible rape are a good example. In raw numbers, approximately 4,200 fewer blacks than whites were arrested for the crime (12,419 versus 16,683). But the proportion of black arrests was 42 percent, almost 30 percent higher than African Americans' representation in the general population. The arrest figures for criminal homicide show an even more pronounced overrepresentation: 56 percent of the 14,104 offenders arrested were black. For the other violent index crimes, aggravated assault and robbery, the proportion of blacks arrested was nearly 39 percent and 59 percent, respectively.

The question of why African Americans are over-represented in crime has long occupied sociologists, criminologists, policymakers, and ordinary Americans alike. Frequently, the debate has generated more heat than light, as the question involves many hot-button subjects: America's racist past, the existence and extent of racism today, presumed cultural differences between blacks and whites.

Many ordinary Americans look for simple, and simplistic, explanations. Obviously, no reasonably informed

Playing on a Stereotype

Robert Harris, Charles Stuart, Jesse Anderson, and Susan Smith never met one another. But the four white Americans have a lot in common.

In January 1996 Harris and his fiancée were shot in Baltimore. Harris described his assailant as an African-American man wearing black and white pants and a camouflage jacket. Though he survived his wounds, his fiancée died at the scene.

Stuart was involved in a similar case in Boston. Police received an emergency call from a hysterical-sounding Stuart, who was calling on his car cell phone. On the way home from childbirth classes with his wife, Stuart said, he had taken a wrong turn and ended up in a bad neighborhood. There he and his wife had been shot. When police finally located Stuart's car, in Boston's predominantly African-American Mission Hill section, it was too late to save his wife and unborn child. But Stuart survived his gunshot wound and in a police lineup identified a black man named Willie Bennett as "looking most like" the shooter.

Tragedy struck outside a suburban Milwaukee restaurant in April 1992. There, Jesse Anderson told police, two black men attacked him and his wife. Anderson survived, but his wife died from multiple stab wounds.

Susan Smith, a young South Carolina mother, also had a chilling story to tell police: she'd been carjacked by a young black male, who had thrown her out of the vehicle and driven off with her two children, ages three and 14 months, in the backseat. With Smith's help, police completed and circulated a composite sketch of the suspect, and federal and state law enforcement officials initiated a nine-day search throughout African-American communities. In the days following the October 1994 crime, Smith also appeared on national television to plead for the lives of her sons.

Harris, Stuart, Anderson, Smith—four white people from different parts of the country who lost loved ones to violent crime. As it turned out, however, the four had something more shocking in common: each had actually committed the crime, fabricating the stories of black assailants to cover their person would suggest that all crime stems from a single cause, but many people do argue that higher rates of criminality among blacks have relatively straightforward explanations. Many, for example, see the issue of race and crime as primarily an economic question: poverty, they feel, strongly contributes to crime, and blacks are overrepresented among America's poor.

Others—influenced, perhaps, by persistent images of African-American criminals such as Willie Horton—suggest that blacks are, for genetic or cultural reasons,

tracks. Harris eventually confessed to hiring a white hit man to kill his fiancée and to shoot him nonfatally. Stuart committed suicide before police could arrest him; he had shot his wife and himself in the car, then given the gun to his brother, who was in another car. Anderson was convicted of first-degree murder in the death of his wife. Police had become suspicious after learning that he had called his wife's insurance company one month before the killing to confirm that her life insurance policy was still in effect, and blood evidence linked him to the crime. Smith finally confessed to pushing her car, with her two sons inside, into a lake; the boys drowned.

Why did these four murderers blame their own crimes on black men? Did they think that would make their stories more believable? Or had they, like many Americans, subconsciously assimilated the "black man as criminal" stereotype?

Sadly, racial hoaxes—as researchers have termed cases in which crimes are falsely blamed on members of other races—do more than reflect society's image of the black man as criminal. They also help create that image. In *The Color of Crime*, author Katheryn K. Russell documented 51 cases of racial hoaxes blaming fictitious black criminals between 1987 and 1996. Russell believes that young children are especially affected by these cases. Referring to the Charles Stuart case, which received an incredible amount of publicity, she writes, "For [children], hearing about the horrible Black man who shot an innocent White man and killed his pregnant wife and unborn baby made the *criminalblackman* imprint indelible—the myth was created." Evidence of this may be found in the case of a seven-year-old girl in Maine who fabricated a story that she had been assaulted by a black man.

Given the damage that racial hoaxes can do, Russell suggests that people who perpetrate them should receive punishment beyond what is specified for giving false information to the police. At least one jurisdiction, the state of New Jersey, has considered legislation making the commission of a racial hoax a felony.

Police stand over the body of a shooting victim, New York City. Gun-related violence claimed the lives of so many young African-American men during the late 1980s and early 1990s that officials declared a national health crisis. A New England Journal of Medicine article estimated that a resident of rural Bangladesh had a greater chance of surviving to age 40 than did a black male in Harlem.

more prone to criminal behavior. Needless to say, this is an extremely controversial view.

In 1994, political scientist Charles Murray and psychologist Richard Herrnstein ignited a firestorm of controversy with the publication of their book *The Bell Curve: Intelligence and Class Structure in American Life.* Murray and Herrnstein linked criminality with intelligence and maintained that African-American crime rates are higher—and will always be higher—because of blacks' lower average intelligence when compared with other races (as evidenced, the authors claimed, by scores on tests of cognitive ability). Essentially these researchers were arguing that race causes crime.

Scholars rushed to criticize Murray and Herrnstein's methodology and their conclusions. The findings of countless studies undercut the "criminal gene" thesis, and even Murray and Herrnstein's main premise, that blacks *are* on average less intelligent than members of other races, is by no means widely accepted. Various factors, including cultural biases, the expectations of test administrators, and the motivation of test-takers, may skew the results of IQ tests. And Murray and Herrnstein failed to consider the effects of educational disadvantages suffered by previous generations of blacks.

If Murray and Herrnstein's work implies that race causes crime, other writers appear to subscribe to the notion that crime causes racism. Political scientist James Q. Wilson, in his book *The Moral Sense*, suggests that the way to reduce white racism is to reduce the level of black crime at least to the level of white crime, which, he goes on to note, "is itself too high." In *The End of Racism*, political scientist Dinesh D'Souza argues that a taxi driver who refuses to pick up a black male fare isn't a racist but rather a good sociologist, given the fact that crime statistics indicate that black males are disproportionately involved in robberies and homicides.

Law-abiding African Americans are painfully aware of the defensive actions that many whites take during chance encounters in stores, on the streets, and in elevators. For some whites it is almost instinctive to clutch their purses, take the next elevator, or look for signs of shoplifting when around blacks. In his book *The Rage of a Privileged Class*, Ellis Cose discusses how such reactions lead to deep-seated anger among middle-class African Americans. If race is assumed to be a cause of crime, and if racism is justified as the result of crime, how can any black person hope to viewed without suspicion?

RACE AND PLACE: RACE AND THE CAUSES OF CRIME

On April 19, 1989, a young woman was found unconscious and badly beaten in the woods of New York City's Central Park. The victim, a white investment banker in her twenties, had been jogging in the park after dark when a group of working- and lower-class black and Hispanic youths aged 14 to 18 attacked her. They beat her unconscious with a lead pipe, gang-raped her, then left her for dead.

The incident, which became known as the Central Park jogger case, received massive media coverage. Readers and viewers were shocked and outraged by the brutality of the crime and the apparently nonchalant attitude of the young perpetrators, who had attacked nine other persons on the same night. News stories frequently used animal imagery, such as "wolf pack" and "herd," in describing those accused of the crime. And the case introduced many Americans to a new term supposedly in use among urban youth: "wilding," which was said to describe the act of searching for random vic-

Researchers have found that an urban setting, poverty, unemployment, and general family disruption are among the factors that contribute to increased rates of violent crime.

53

Anton McCray, one of the minority youths convicted in the beating and gang rape of a white jogger in Central Park, is accompanied by black activist Al Sharpton. Was race a cause of the brutal crime? The media repeatedly asked this question.

tims to rape, rob, or murder, seemingly as an almost recreational activity.

With a well-to-do white victim and a gang of minority perpetrators, it was perhaps inevitable that the question would be asked as to what role race had played. A study of media coverage of the incident over a 15-day period, from April 20 to May 5, revealed that the five newspapers and six television stations examined cited race as a possible explanation for the crime 54 times, more than twice that of any other factor. Although the majority of the news stories that mentioned race went on to deny its relevance, 20 percent of the stories suggested that race was a potential cause of the crime.

Does race in fact cause crime? Undoubtedly this question was asked, even subconsciously, by many people who heard or read about the Central Park jogger case. Undoubtedly it continues to be asked by people who are acquainted with statistics showing that a disproportionate number of African Americans, especially young males, commit crimes of violence.

A few researchers (such as Murray and Herrnstein) have attempted to correlate higher rates of black criminality with genetic or cultural characteristics unique to African Americans. However, despite the popular appeal of such theories, which reduce complex phenomena to simple explanations, most criminologists have concluded that the causes of crime are multiple. What's more, conditions that tend to increase criminality among African Americans seem to have the same effect on other racial and ethnic groups.

In the roughly two centuries that crime causation has been systematically studied, numerous theories have been advanced to explain crime across time, place, and cultural group. It is far beyond the scope of this book to address all such theories. Rather, the focus here will be on examining theories that might account for disproportionate black criminality in the United States.

Social scientists have found that certain factors are predictive of higher rates of crime, particularly violent crime. One such factor is city residence. Urban neighborhoods, whether occupied by minorities or nonminorities, tend to have higher crime rates than nonurban neighborhoods. This holds true both in the United States and abroad, for cities as diverse as Los Angeles and Liverpool, England. Other factors found to predict higher rates of violent crime include joblessness, poverty, female-headed families, and general family disruption.

Research by well-known sociologists Robert Sampson, of the University of Chicago, and William Julius Wilson, now at Harvard University, found that these same factors are associated with higher rates of violent crime (especially robbery) among both blacks and

When mainstream goals such as wealth and status seem unattainable by socially accepted means, some people will adopt deviant values or criminal behaviors.

whites. However, Sampson and Wilson and other researchers have also demonstrated that even among the poor, blacks and whites don't share equally disadvantaged worlds. African Americans' overrepresentation within crime statistics is consistent with (and in some areas, surpassed by) their overrepresentation within statistics for poverty and other negative social conditions, such as unemployment, homelessness, infant mortality, and substandard housing.

Statistics compiled by the U.S. Bureau of the Census for the years 1980 through 1995 confirm the tremendous—and persistent—differences across race. In 1980, for example, only 6.9 percent of white families were reported as living below the poverty line, compared with 27.8 percent of black families. By 1995 the percentage of white families living in poverty had risen to 9.1, but the figure for black families was still three times higher, at 27.3 percent.

The figures for unrelated individuals living below the poverty line were even starker. In 1980, the percentage of unrelated black persons living below the poverty line was 31.0 percent; the percentage of white persons similarly situated, 9.0 percent. The gap hadn't narrowed much by 1995, with 30.6 percent of black persons and 11.7 percent of white persons living in poverty.

Perhaps not surprisingly, unemployment figures for 1995 paint a similarly disparate picture across race. In that year the reported percentage of unemployed blacks was more than twice that of whites. For black males, the figure stood at 10.6 percent, compared with 4.9 percent for white males; 10.2 percent of black females, and 4.8 percent of white females, were unemployed. Within certain age categories, the disparity was even more pronounced. For example, the percentage of unemployed black males age 16 to 19 was reported at 37.1 percent; the percentage of unemployed black females in the same age group was 34.3 percent. For their white counterparts, the figures were 15.6 percent and 13.4 percent, respectively.

Statistics detailing the percentages of individuals who are unemployed or living in poverty don't tell the full story, however. Unemployment and poverty alone are less predictive of a person's chances of criminality than are the overall social and economic characteristics of the community in which the person lives. Other factors being equal, a poor, unemployed person living in a predominantly middle-class suburban neighborhood or in a rural area is less likely to be involved in crime than is a poor, unemployed person living in a dilapidated urban neighborhood. Abundant evidence suggests that differences in crime rates are not primarily a matter of race, but of place. For historical, social, and economic reasons, however, blacks are most likely to live in the kinds of communities that produce higher rates of criminality.

In the United States, systematic study of the complex connections between race, crime, poverty, and place of residence was largely pioneered by the sociologists Clifford Shaw and Henry McKay. The results of their studies in Chicago, initially reported in 1942, pointed to the conclusion that the different rates at which blacks and whites committed crimes could be explained in large part by the different environments in which blacks and whites lived. Additionally, blacks' environments tended to produce patterns of behavior that whites then mistakenly viewed as cultural traits of African Americans in general.

More recently, sociologists Robert Sampson and William Julius Wilson have pursued similar lines of inquiry. Their research suggests that, while the issue is painfully complex, involving numerous interrelated factors, Shaw and McKay's thesis—that the higher rate of black criminality can be attributed to environmental factors—remains valid.

In their essay "Toward a Theory of Race, Crime and Urban Inequality," Sampson and Wilson ask the question "To what extent are blacks as a group differentially exposed to criminogenic [crime-producing] structural conditions?" In response, they offer the following observations:

- In 1980, 70 percent of all poor non-Hispanic whites lived in nonpoverty areas (areas where less than 20 percent of the residents live below the poverty line) in the 10 largest U.S. central cities, while only 16 percent of poor blacks did.
- Overall, less than 7 percent of poor whites lived in extreme poverty or ghetto areas; by contrast, 38 percent of poor blacks lived in such areas. In New York City, for example, 70 percent of poor blacks live in poverty neighborhoods (where 20 percent or more of the residents have incomes below the poverty line), and 70 percent of poor whites live in nonpoverty neighborhoods.
- The majority of poor blacks live in communities characterized by high rates of family disruption, whereas the majority of poor whites, even those from "broken homes," live in areas of relative family stability.

The extent of the difference across race is shocking. For their research, Sampson and Wilson wanted to find cities where the proportion of blacks living in poverty was equal to or less than the proportion of whites, and where the proportion of black families with children

headed by a single parent was equal to or less than that
for white families. Examining race-specific census data
on the 171 largest U.S. cities, they found that there
wasn't a single city with a population over 100,000 in
which "blacks live in ecological equality with whites
when it comes to these basic features of economic and
family organization." Furthermore, in their estimation
"[r]acial differences in poverty and family disruption are
so strong that the 'worst' urban contexts in which
whites reside are considerably better than the average
context of black communities." In other words, a major
difference between poor whites and poor blacks is that
poor whites tend to live among other people who are
not poor and who have stable families, whereas poor
blacks tend to be trapped in communities of *concentrated* poverty and family instability.

Thus, Sampson and Wilson conclude, "More than
40 years after Shaw and McKay's assessment of race and
urban ecology, we still cannot say that blacks and
whites share a similar environment—especially with
regard to concentrated urban poverty." And crime and
disorder overwhelmingly plague communities characterized by concentrated poverty.

In 1992 stunning evidence of this phenomenon
emerged from research conducted on New York State's
prison population. Three-quarters of the state's entire
prison population, which was 85 percent black and
Hispanic, came from just seven New York City neighborhoods. Those neighborhoods (the Lower East Side,
the South Bronx, Harlem, Brownsville, Bedford-
Stuyvesant, East New York, and South Jamaica)
encompass only 18 of the state's 150 Assembly districts
and only 12 percent of the state's total population. U.S.
census and local government data confirm that they
are among New York's poorest neighborhoods and are
composed primarily of African-American and Hispanic
residents.

By way of example, the 1990 census recorded that

81 percent of the residents in the Brownsville section of Brooklyn were black and 17 percent were Hispanic. The median household income was about $15,000. More than one-third of all the families were receiving public assistance, and 37 percent were living below the poverty line. Not surprisingly, fewer than 6 percent of Brownsville's nearly 85,000 residents were enrolled in college. The neighborhood also had the highest unemployment rate in New York City for males over age 16. And Brownsville had one of the highest murder rates of any New York City community, along with high rates of robbery, assault, burglary, and theft.

If the evidence links higher rates of black criminality with residency in communities characterized by concentrated poverty, the next question becomes, how do these communities spawn criminal behavior? Sampson and Wilson try to answer that question. They have developed a theory of criminality among poverty-stricken urban blacks that incorporates both environmental (that is, structural) and cultural explanations. The theory as proposed is not intended or expected to apply to blacks in other contexts. Like whites, Sampson and Wilson note, blacks and other ethnic minorities are not all the same.

Under Sampson and Wilson's "urban inequality theory," environmental conditions within a socially disorganized community, such as concentrated poverty and social isolation, give rise (among a small number of residents) to behavioral adaptations and thought patterns that run counter to those considered typical of mainstream society. These thought patterns and behaviors tend to be conducive to crime. In poverty-stricken, socially disorganized urban neighborhoods, communication between residents is impeded by factors such as mutual distrust, anonymity, and institutional instability. And residents have limited access to mainstream goals (such as property ownership and the acquisition of wealth). The result is that no commu-

nity consensus exists regarding what is and is not acceptable behavior, and a small portion of the residents will engage in crime.

Other studies also support the assertion that structurally disorganized communities tend to spawn value systems and attitudes that tolerate crime and deviance. For example, in his 1978 study of a bar in a black ghetto of Chicago's South Side, sociologist Elijah Anderson found that mainstream societal values coexisted with the values associated with so-called deviant subcultures. Not unlike the apparent values of many urban neighborhoods today, these values included "toughness," "getting big money," "going for bad," and "having fun." Because of limited mainstream opportunities, lower-class residents, in Anderson's analysis, "create

Police arrest white youths who started a brawl during a parade. Researchers have found that the same social and economic conditions that lead to increased criminality among blacks also lead to increased criminality among whites—strong evidence against the hypothesis that African Americans are genetically or culturally predisposed to crime.

their own particular standards of conduct along variant lines open to them." In this context, the use of violence, for example, is not valued as a primary goal of behavior but is nonetheless *expected* and *tolerated* as a fact of life. Anderson even suggests that in certain community contexts, access to the means of achieving mainstream goals and exposure to wider cultural values are so extremely limited that such values are simply not relevant—they become "unviable." Such an outlook fosters feelings of hopelessness, which in turn facilitates the adoption of criminal values and behaviors.

Sampson and Wilson point out that, in particular, youngsters in inner-city ghetto neighborhoods "are more likely to witness violent acts, to be taught to be violent by exhortation, and to have role models who do not adequately control their own violent impulses or restrain their own anger." In short, they are more likely to see violence as a way of life.

Behavioral patterns that run counter to mainstream values are most likely to be transmitted from one generation to the next when a particular community or group of communities is socially isolated from the dominant culture (through poverty or patterns of segregation based on race or ethnicity). The absence of sustained contact with people and institutions that represent mainstream society means that the values of mainstream society are much less likely to be passed on. In their place, according to Sampson and Wilson, a system of values will tend to emerge whereby "crime, disorder, and drug use are less than fervently condemned and hence expected as part of everyday life." And the sociologists note that such "social perceptions and tolerances, in turn, appear to influence the probability of crime."

Many factors contribute to the process, and often their influences are subtle, indirect, and interconnected. For example, in research reported in the late 1980s, Sampson explored the connections between

black male joblessness, economic deprivation, and family disruption. He found that the prevalence of female-headed families in black communities was directly related to the scarcity of employed black men relative to black women. In turn, subsequent research found that black family disruption was substantially related to rates of black murder and robbery, particularly among juveniles.

Once again, however, research has shown that the same factors affect rates of violent behavior among whites. As Sampson and Wilson note, "Despite a tremendous difference in mean levels of family disruption among black and white communities, the percentage of white families headed by a female also [has] a large . . . effect on white juvenile and white adult violence." They conclude, therefore, that "the effect of black family disruption on black crime . . . [cannot] be attributed to unique cultural factors within the black

In poor urban communities, fear and social isolation impede communication among residents, and as a result there is no consensus regarding what is and is not acceptable behavior. This, in turn, appears to increase the probability of crime.

community given the similar effect of white family disruption on white crime."

Research reported in 1997 by sociologists Liqun Cao, Anthony Adams, and Vickie Jensen also refutes the notion that blacks are culturally more prone to violence. In their study, the researchers failed to find a significant difference between white and black males with regard to willingness to initiate the use of violence. In contrast, however, white males were found to be "significantly more vocal than Blacks in expressing violent tendenc[ies] in defensive situations." Further support for this proposition may be contained in arrest statistics for 1994. While the number of blacks arrested for murder/nonnegligent manslaughter and robbery exceeds the number of whites by roughly 3,000 and 30,000 respectively, the number of whites arrested for aggravated assault and "other" assaults exceeds the number of blacks arrested for such offenses by roughly 90,000 and 290,000 respectively.

The fact that higher rates of black criminality can't be adequately explained by cultural characteristics unique to African Americans points the finger back to the role that American social structure plays in contributing to black criminality. And, as chapter 2 detailed, the role of legal history in shaping the existing social structure cannot be ignored. Indeed, perhaps the question we should be asking is not Does race cause crime? but Does racism cause crime?

At first blush, many would answer no, arguing that the disproportionate number of African Americans now living in areas of concentrated urban poverty and social disorder can be attributed to factors beyond the control of government policymakers. And, in fact, there is some merit to this argument. America's shift from an industrial, manufacturing-oriented economy to a postindustrial, service- and information-oriented economy has meant the loss of hundreds of thousands of blue-collar jobs, especially in the older cities. In addition, the large-scale movement of whites and middle- and upper-income blacks out of central cities and into the suburbs has concentrated minorities with the fewest economic means in poor urban neighborhoods. This, of course, has had a whole range of profound consequences, including declining property values, shrinking tax bases, and underfunded schools—which themselves accelerate the isolation and physical and economic decline of the neighborhoods, and thus tend to increase crime.

But if market forces have played a large part in relegating a significant percentage of African Americans to concentrated-poverty areas, the role of intentional policy decisions cannot be discounted either. For example, beginning in the 1950s and continuing into the 1970s, municipalities razed a significant portion of the country's inner-city housing stock in the name of "urban renewal." This had a huge impact on African Americans (one source says that 20 percent of all central-city private housing units occupied by blacks nationwide were lost between 1960 and 1970 alone). Accompanying the loss of low-income private housing was the creation of government-subsidized public housing for the economically disadvantaged. One of the most significant effects of public housing projects was to further concentrate the poor and minorities in economically depressed areas. Some observers believe that this was an unintended consequence of an essentially benevolent policy. Others disagree. For example, researchers Adam Bickford and Douglas S. Massey argue that "public housing is a federally funded, physically permanent institution for the isolation of black families by race and class." Whatever the intentions of policymakers, a large body of research and statistics indicates that nowhere is the urban crime problem more pronounced than in housing projects.

Another way in which government has been implicated in contributing to crime is through neighborhood

At play in a vacant lot in Detroit. Although concentrated poverty and family disruption increase crime among people of all races, two prominent sociologists claim that "the 'worst' urban contexts in which whites reside are considerably better than the average context of black communities."

deterioration caused by lax enforcement of city housing codes and inadequate policies on code enforcement and repair of city properties by urban landlords. The strong negative impact of such failures has been especially well documented in Chicago and New York (for example, by Arnold R. Hirsch in the 1983 work *Making the Second Ghetto: Race and Housing in Chicago, 1940–1960*).

Urban communities have also suffered from the consequences of local political decisions to withdraw city municipal services for public health and fire safety—and poorer neighborhoods have arguably suffered the most. In analyzing the "planned shrinkage" of New York City's fire and health services, for example, health policy researchers Rodrick Wallace and Deborah Wallace observed, "The consequences of withdrawing municipal services from poor neighborhoods, the resulting outbreaks of contagious urban decay and forced migration which shred essential social networks and cause social disintegration, have become a highly significant contributor to decline in public health [and increase in crime] among the poor."

According to Sampson and Wilson, such shrinkage may have a circular effect. That is, the loss of social integration and social networks caused by cutbacks in such services may increase behavioral patterns of violence, and that, in turn, further disrupts social networks and causes further social disintegration. On the other hand, it has also been suggested that the reduction of emergency services in particular increases the likelihood that incidents that in other neighborhoods would be nonlethal, in these neighborhoods will result in death. To some extent, therefore, the lack of adequate services may help to account for the overrepresentation of blacks within both the offender and victim categories of murder/nonnegligent manslaughter, while whites are significantly more involved in acts of aggravated assault and other assaults that don't result in death.

Disordered conditions in the places where a significant proportion of African Americans live, work, and raise their families may go a long way toward explaining why disproportionate numbers of blacks are involved in crime. But disordered conditions don't fully explain why so many blacks are arrested and incarcerated. Other factors are also at work, and in many ways these factors are even more disturbing.

Presumed Guilty? Race and the Police

ecause urban neighborhoods with concentrated poverty produce more crime, it might be reasonable to expect increased police activity in these neighborhoods. And because disproportionate numbers of blacks live in concentrated-poverty areas, logically they would, as a group, have more contacts with the police. This might partially explain why African Americans are arrested disproportionately even for crimes, such as drug abuse, that they don't commit disproportionately: more police attention means a greater possibility that criminal activity will be detected.

However, statistics as well as anecdotal evidence suggest that frequent police contacts aren't limited to blacks who are poor and living in urban centers. In fact, some observers believe that *all* African Americans are treated differently by law enforcement (and that whites involved in crime are less likely to be caught given this differential treatment). Individual police

Miami police subdue a black youth during a riot, May 17, 1980. The riot erupted after four police officers were acquitted in the beating death of African-American insurance executive Arthur McDuffie. McDuffie had originally been stopped for traffic violations.

69

officers and even entire departments, these observers feel, seem to have bought into the notion that blacks as a group are a dangerous, criminal element.

One law enforcement practice that has angered African-American leaders and civil rights activists of all racial and ethnic backgrounds is called racial profiling. Essentially the practice is a variation of a law enforcement technique that has been accepted for years. Profiling is an investigatory tool whereby behavioral experts generate, and police officers are given, a description of the expected characteristics of someone who committed a specific crime or who may be engaged in a particular kind of criminal activity—absent an eyewitness description or other evidence implicating an individual. Profiling has proved especially useful in the investigation of serial murder.

However, some police departments have adopted—either formally or informally—the practice of race-based profiling. This practice assumes that people of color are more likely to be involved in crime, and use of the technique potentially exposes any African American or Hispanic to unwarranted police scrutiny. Many state police departments especially have been accused of racial profiling in stopping motorists along turnpikes and freeways. For example, state police in New Jersey might feel that the "typical" profile of an interstate cocaine carrier is an African American or Hispanic in an expensive, late-model car with Florida plates. (Florida is a major point of importation for cocaine.) Seeing someone who fit that description, a state police officer would make a traffic stop, detain and question the individual, then ask to search the vehicle. The courts have ruled that when such stops are based on race and the officer has no probable cause (defined roughly as facts that make something more likely than not) to believe a crime has been committed, this practice is illegal. But it seems to be widespread anyway.

Indeed, many blacks have reported that *anytime*

they are in a car, especially an expensive one, they receive extra police scrutiny. So common are unwarranted traffic stops, African Americans say sardonically, that their "offense" might best be described as DWB—"driving while black." Anecdotal evidence seems to support this claim. For example, the television newsmagazine *20/20* conducted an experiment in 1992, in which two groups of young men—one white, the other black—were sent out over several evenings in Los Angeles. The young men drove identical cars and took the same routes at the same time of day. Whereas the black men were stopped and questioned by police on several occasions in one evening, the white drivers were not, even though they saw police cars pass them by 16 different times.

The issue of racial profiling on the nation's highways

U.S. marshals raid a crack house, Washington, D.C. Part of the reason blacks are arrested disproportionately, even for crimes they don't commit disproportionately, may be that law enforcement efforts tend to be concentrated in the poor urban neighborhoods where many blacks live.

has drawn a great deal of attention recently, and changes in police procedures may be in the works. In New Jersey, for example, the chief of the state police department was forced to resign in 1999 when allegations of widespread racial profiling by state police officers surfaced. Roughly five years earlier, similar allegations had resulted in a lawsuit that the state police and the public defenders office eventually settled. There is strong evidence that the Maryland State Police also still use racial profiling, despite a lawsuit that cost that department $100,000 to settle. An internal state police document uncovered in the course of the lawsuit stated, "The [drug] dealers and couriers are predominantly black males and females." Other racial-profiling lawsuits have been filed against jurisdictions as widely distributed as Chicago; Eagle County, Colorado; Pittsburgh; Gloucester Township, New Jersey; and Volusia County, Florida.

But stopping African-American motorists on the highways is only one manifestation of racial profiling. Police sometimes conduct "sweeps" of buses or trains, during which they question certain commuters and ask to search their baggage. For the most part, the police are looking for drugs. Again, however, these bus and train sweeps seem to target blacks and Hispanics almost exclusively. In an examination of 55 reported federal bus and train search cases from January 1, 1993, to August 22, 1995, the race or ethnicity of the subjects detained and questioned was found to be as follows: 36 blacks, 11 Hispanics, 6 whites, 1 Asian, and 1 Filipino. Minority pedestrians and bicyclists in the Beverly Hills and Hollywood areas of California have also complained of discriminatory stops.

Many observers argue that if African Americans are singled out for extra law enforcement scrutiny, they are also subject to higher levels of force in encounters with police. Police experts say that situational variables— such as location (high- or low-crime area) and the suspect's perceived criminal involvement, demeanor, and social status—dictate how much force an officer will use. It is therefore difficult if not impossible to prove that blacks are intentionally treated with higher levels of force than whites under similar circumstances. (It is interesting to note, however, that all the above variables would tend to put blacks at more risk, regardless of their individual character.) But again, there is enough anecdotal evidence of bias to raise questions in the minds of many people:

• On February 4, 1999, four New York City police officers shot to death an unarmed 22-year-old West African man, Amadou Diallo, in the doorway of his Bronx home. Apparently the officers wanted to question Diallo because he resembled the sketch of a serial rapist who was operating in the area. (He turned out not to be the rapist.) The officers claimed that they believed Diallo was reaching for a gun, but it appears he was reaching for his wallet—which was found inches away from his outstretched hand—perhaps for identification. What made the shooting so controversial was the extreme level of force used, in a multifamily residential building to boot: the four police officers fired a total of 41 shots from their high-powered 9 mm handguns; two of the officers completely emptied the 16-round clips. Police dubbed the killing a tragic mistake.

• In 1996 James Consalvo, a New Brunswick, New Jersey, police officer, shot to death an African-American woman suspected of being a prostitute after she bit his finger and refused to let go. Although the woman, Carolyn Adams, was unarmed, the officer claimed to have been in fear for his life. A grand jury refused to indict him for the shooting, and he later retired from the force with a $37,000 pension.

- In Pittsburgh, police stopped black motorist Jonny Gammage on October 12, 1995, for a traffic violation. He was driving a late-model Jaguar belonging to his cousin, a professional football player. According to the officers, when Gammage was ordered out of the car, he emerged holding a cell phone that one of the officers mistook for a gun. Three police officers forced him to the ground, and the weight of the officers pressing on his back and neck prevented him from breathing. Gammage died of asphyxiation. One officer, John Votjas, was tried for the killing, but he was acquitted amid charges that the prosecution's efforts had been halfhearted.
- On December 22, 1994, New York City police officer Francis X. Livoti put Anthony Baez in a choke hold that had been outlawed by the police department, triggering a fatal asthma attack. The incident had begun when a football accidentally hit a police cruiser. In a nonjury trial for criminally negligent homicide, Livoti was acquitted, even though Judge Gerald Sheindlin called the death of Anthony Baez "tragic, unnecessary and avoidable."
- In 1989 Clement Lloyd, a 23-year-old black motorcyclist whom Miami police were chasing for speeding and reckless driving, was shot and killed by Officer William Lozano. When Lozano heard over his police radio that the chase was headed in his direction, he waited and shot Lloyd in the head as he rode by. A passenger on the motorcycle also died from injuries sustained in the ensuing crash.
- On October 29, 1984, Eleanor Bumpurs, a 67-year-old African-American woman described as 270 pounds and arthritic, was shot to death while resisting eviction from her New York City apartment. Bumpurs had not been given notice that

she was one month behind on her rent; in fact, there is some question that she actually owed the $96.85. Nonetheless, three police officers arrived to evict her. They had riot shields, a restraining pole, and a shotgun, and they may have been told that Bumpurs had a history of mental illness. In the course of the encounter, Bumpurs twice avoided being caught by the restraining pole, and she brandished a knife. The officer with the shotgun, Stephen Sullivan, fired, blowing off part of the woman's hand and making it impossible, according to prosecutors' files, for her to hold the knife. But Sullivan pumped the shotgun and fired again, killing Bumpurs. Both the mayor and police commissioner of New York City characterized the shooting as "legal," although the commissioner, Benjamin Ward, later admitted that Bumpurs should not have died. Sullivan was tried for manslaughter in early 1987, but he was acquitted.

• In December 1979 a 33-year-old black insurance executive, Arthur McDuffie, was beaten to death by police in Miami, Florida. McDuffie had been stopped for traffic violations after a high-speed chase and was severely beaten by as many as five policemen. At the officers' trial for murder, the medical examiner, who had performed more than 3,500 autopsies in his career, testified that McDuffie had sustained the worst brain damage he had ever seen. Nonetheless, the all-white jury took less than three hours to return not guilty verdicts on all counts.

In each of the preceding cases, police used deadly force against an African American or Hispanic in the course of what began as a rather routine encounter: the questioning of a possible suspect, an attempted eviction, a traffic stop, accidental damage to a police

Ray Seals (right), accompanied by Pittsburgh Steelers teammates Greg Lloyd (left) and Brentson Buckner, attends a memorial rally for his cousin Jonny Gammage. Gammage was driving Seals's car on October 12, 1995, when a traffic stop by Pittsburgh police ended in his tragic death. Such incidents, critics charge, are far too common.

cruiser, the arrest of an unarmed woman. None of the suspects had committed a violent felony, and while some of the officers involved cited their fear of the suspect, under the circumstances it is difficult to find a reasonable basis for such fears. Could it be that the officers were reacting in part to the suspects' race? That the fact they were black led the officers to feel, perhaps on a subconscious level, that the suspects were more dangerous and inherently more criminal?

James Fyfe, a criminal justice professor at Temple University and himself a former New York City police officer, has asked whether the police have two trigger fingers, one for whites and another for Hispanics and blacks. Other researchers have found evidence that the answer to this question might be yes. Samuel Walker, Cassia Spohn, and Miriam DeLone note in their 1996 book, *The Color of Justice,* that "historically, the police have shot and killed far more African-Americans than Whites." (The reported ratio for 1970, for example, was seven blacks shot and killed for every white.) A study of the Chicago police found that between 1974 and 1978 Hispanics were about twice as likely as whites to be shot and killed by police, and blacks were twice as likely as Hispanics to die in that manner. A similar pattern was found in Los Angeles and New York City in research reported in 1992.

Some researchers have attempted to explain the racial disparity by accounting for nonracial variables. For example, in a 1981 study William A. Geller and Kevin J. Karales examined data on persons shot and killed by Chicago police in 1970, controlling for "at-risk" status (defined as a group's overall arrests for "forcible felonies," including such offenses as murder, rape, armed robbery, aggravated assault, and burglary). Geller and Karales found that when this variable was taken into account, the racial disparity in fatal police shootings disappeared, and in fact whites were shot and killed at a slightly higher rate. (The researchers don't appear to have considered that an arrest is only an accusation of a crime, and a portion of the "forcible felony" suspects shot and killed by the police may have been innocent.) Similarly, police scholar Albert Reiss concluded in 1971 that "class rather than race determines police misconduct." In his book *Police and the Public*, Reiss notes that the typical victim of excessive police force is a lower-class male, regardless of race. One problem with Reiss's conclusion is that it fails to address the question of how police determine the class status of suspects. Do some police automatically perceive African Americans as "lower class"? Was Jonny Gammage perceived that way even though he was driving a late-model Jaguar? Indeed, was the fact that he was driving such an expensive car the reason he was stopped in the first place?

If African Americans face a greater chance than

whites of being killed by police officers, a 1985 Supreme Court decision appears to have at least narrowed the gap. That decision, in the case of *Tennessee v. Garner*, limited the circumstances under which police officers can legally use deadly force.

The facts of the *Garner* case are as follows. Around 10:45 on the night of October 3, 1974, Memphis, Tennessee, police officers Elton Hymon and Leslie Wright responded to a call about a possible prowler. When they arrived at the scene, a woman standing on her porch told them that she had heard breaking glass at the house next door. While his partner radioed the police dispatcher, Hymon went into the backyard to investigate. He saw someone running across the yard. When the suspect stopped at a six-foot-high chain-link fence, Hymon shone his flashlight on him. He was a small African-American male whom the police officer judged to be about 17 or 18 years old (actually the suspect, Edward Garner, was 15). Hymon testified that he was "reasonably sure" the suspect was unarmed (that proved to be correct) and that he didn't believe he presented a risk of harm. Moving toward the suspect, he shouted, "Police! Halt!" but Garner tried to climb the fence, and Hymon shot him fatally in the back of the head. It turned out that during the burglary Garner, an eighth grader, had taken a purse containing $10.

Garner's father sued the Memphis Police Department, claiming that his son's Fourth, Fifth, Sixth, Eighth, and Fourteenth Amendment rights had been violated. The case made its way to the Supreme Court, where it was argued 10 years after Edward Garner's death, on October 30, 1984. In delivering its ruling the following March, the Court sided with Mr. Garner. It found that the shooting had amounted to an unreasonable search and seizure under the Fourth Amendment and a violation of due process under the Fifth and Fourteenth Amendments. The Court also provided guidelines for the use of deadly force by police:

This case requires us to determine the constitutionality of the use of deadly force to prevent the escape of an apparently unarmed suspected felon. We conclude that such force may not be used unless it is necessary to prevent the escape and the officer has probable cause to believe that the suspect poses a significant threat of death or serious physical injury to the officer or others.

Do police have two trigger fingers, one for black suspects and one for white suspects? Statistics suggest that the answer may be yes.

Although the decision said nothing about the race of suspects—and, in fact, Officer Hymon was himself an African American—the result may have been a reduction in the number of blacks shot and killed by police. In Memphis between 1969 and 1974, for example, police had shot and killed 14 people who were categorized as "unarmed and not assaultive"; 13 of them were African Americans. In fact, fully half of the blacks

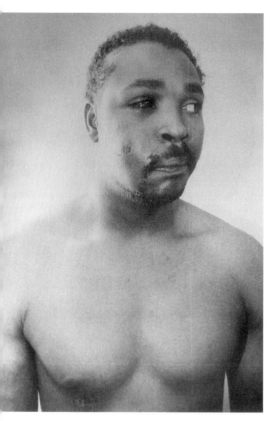

This photo of Rodney King, taken three days after his videotaped beating by Los Angeles police officers, was introduced into evidence at the trial of four white policemen. The acquittal of the officers sparked four days of rioting in Los Angeles.

fatally shot by Memphis police during that period *were* unarmed and not assaultive. After the *Garner* decision, for the period from 1985 to 1989, *no one* who was unarmed and not assaultive was shot by Memphis police. The Supreme Court's ruling required officers to have both probable cause that the suspect had committed a felony *and* a well-founded belief that he or she posed a serious risk of harm. And it seemed that under the previous policy of the Memphis police, which had permitted officers to "use all necessary means to effect the arrest" of a felony suspect, officers had chosen to apply deadly force to unarmed suspects much more frequently when those suspects were black.

Even before the *Garner* decision, however, various police departments around the country—reacting to protests by civil rights groups and to lawsuits—had begun revising their use-of-force policies in the early 1970s to eliminate much of the discretion officers had in applying deadly force. In New York City, for example, Police Commissioner Patrick V. Murphy imposed a "defense of life" rule in 1972. Under this policy, police were permitted to fire at a suspect only when the life of the officer or another person was threatened. As in Memphis after the *Garner* decision, the adoption of defense-of-life rules saved minority lives, and the racial disparity between blacks and whites killed nationally by police declined from 7 to 1 in 1970 to 2.8 to 1 in 1979.

Nationally, the total number of persons fatally shot by police declined from a high of 559 in 1975 to 300 in 1987, in the immediate post-*Garner* period. Data examined by professors Lawrence Sherman and Ellen Cohn suggest that virtually all the lives saved by the more restrictive use-of-force rules were racial minorities, as the number of whites shot and killed remained practically unchanged.

While the *Garner* decision may have gone a long way toward protecting people of color from excessive police force, some observers believe it's still too early to declare the problem solved. They point to such troubling recent cases as those of Anthony Baez, Jonny Gammage, and suspected New Brunswick prostitute Carolyn Adams. None of the officers suffered criminal sanctions for his conduct, despite the fact that none of the victims was a felony suspect, as the *Garner* decision requires to justify the use of deadly force, and arguably none fulfilled *Garner*'s other requirement, that the suspect present a clear danger of serious harm.

The common denominators in these cases seem to be that the victim was a person of color, and that he or she was perceived as being uncooperative with the police. Did jurors and perhaps even judges believe these people "got what they deserved" because they failed to be sufficiently docile during a police encounter?

That same question had been asked, though the circumstances of the case were more complex, in 1991 in the wake of one of the most infamous incidents of apparently excessive police force in American history. On the night of March 3, after an attempted traffic stop on California's Foothill Freeway, black construction worker Rodney King led police on an extended high-speed chase. When Los Angeles police finally managed to stop his car, King initially refused to get out of the vehicle and be handcuffed. Police twice shot him with a Taser "stun gun." Then, while King was on the ground, surrounded by more than a dozen policemen and apparently pleading for mercy, three officers beat him savagely with nightsticks as a sergeant looked on. Commentators would later liken the policemen's conduct to a "feeding frenzy." However, had it not been for a man on a nearby balcony who videotaped the extended beating, the case might quickly have been forgotten. But the two-minute tape was soon airing on television stations throughout the country.

The Supreme Court's 1985 Garner v. Tennessee decision limited the circumstances under which police officers may use deadly force. But in several recent cases police officers have apparently violated the regulations in using deadly force against blacks and Hispanics—and not been punished.

Four officers—the three who administered the beating and the sergeant who stood by and did nothing—were tried for assault in 1992. At trial, the defendants claimed that they had believed King was high on PCP, a drug that makes the user impervious to pain. (He hadn't been, although his blood alcohol level had measured .19, more than double the legal threshold for drunken driving in California.) Defense experts also showed freeze-frame images from the videotape and maintained that the blows delivered—about 89 in all—were consistent with department regulations. To many Americans who had seen the shocking videotaped images, however, it seemed obvious that the police had used excessive force, and it was widely assumed that the officers would be convicted. When the white jury from suburban Simi Valley returned not guilty verdicts on April 29, outrage in the mostly minority community of

South Central Los Angeles erupted into four days of rioting. By the time 10,000 police, National Guard officers, and federal troops had restored order, more than 50 people had been killed and 2,000 injured; approximately 14,000 buildings had been burned, looted, or vandalized; and property damage was estimated at almost $1 billion.

Besides the obvious impact on South Central Los Angeles, many observers believe that the acquittal of the officers in the Rodney King case had a corrosive effect on the justice system. Some observers similarly feel that the failure to punish the officers who killed Jonny Gammage, Anthony Baez, and Carolyn Adams could also prove harmful. First of all, such cases might encourage the use of excessive force against minorities by other officers, who might assume that they won't have to answer for their conduct. Second, the failure to punish unlawful police behavior against minorities validates the view of some officers that minorities as a group are dangerous and undeserving of all the protections accorded whites. And third, minority distrust of police and the justice system as a whole is reinforced, leading to an adversarial attitude between the police and the communities they are supposed to protect.

The results of two polls, one of law enforcement professionals and the other of ordinary citizens, hint at the enormous perception of police bias. In a survey of 650 Los Angeles Police Department officers, 25 percent of the respondents agreed with the statement that "racial bias (prejudice) on the part of officers toward minority citizens currently exists and contributes to a negative interaction between police and the community." A *New York Times* poll found that well over half of black citizens, 58 percent, viewed the police as corrupt.

FAIR TREATMENT? RACE AND PROSECUTION

T he year 1994 was something of a milestone for the American justice system. In that year, for the first time ever, the U.S. prison population exceeded one million. In arriving at that mark, America had seen explosive growth in its incarceration rate: the number of federal and state prison inmates had more than doubled in just 10 years. And, according to the Bureau of Justice Statistics (BJS), during the first six months of 1994 alone, prison population growth proceeded at a rate that would fill three new 500-bed prisons every week.

What drove this growth was not so much more crime—though crime rates had risen during the 1980s—but more severe punishments for criminals. Widespread public fear of, and anger toward, violent criminals, along with perceptions that the illegal drug trade was out of control, spurred legislators to enact new laws stiffening criminal penalties, supposedly for society's most dangerous offenders.

Like the people shown here, most crack users are white. Yet the overwhelming majority of those serving prison sentences for crack offenses are black. A large part of the reason, it seems, is that prosecutors are more likely to aggressively prosecute African Americans.

Not surprisingly, given arrest rates disproportionate to their numbers in the general population, blacks contributed significantly to the overall astonishing growth in incarceration. In fact, according to BJS, in 1994 blacks were incarcerated at a rate of 1,432 per 100,000 black U.S. residents; by contrast, there were only 203 white inmates per 100,000 white residents. Blacks' rate of incarceration in 1994 was *seven times* that of whites, a differential, BJS reported, that continued the pattern of previous years.

All other things being equal, one would expect the different rates of incarceration for blacks and whites to mirror their respective shares of total arrests, or at least arrests for serious crimes. Interestingly, a comparison of incarceration rates along with arrest statistics contained in the Uniform Crime Reports for 1994 (or any other recent year, for that matter) indicates that the relative proportions of blacks and whites incarcerated does *not* match the relative proportions arrested. The incarceration rate for blacks is significantly higher. For example, the UCR records a total of 11,848,833 reported arrests in 1994, and whites were charged in 7,894,414, or 66.5 percent, of the cases. Black arrests totaled 3,705,713, or just 31.3 percent. For the index crimes, the proportions were similar: whites accounted for 61.4 percent, blacks 33.1 percent of the total.

Even with the violent index crimes, in which African Americans' disproportion is notably high, whites still accounted for a larger percentage of arrests, 53.4 percent to 44.7 percent. Whites comprised 75.1 percent of the arson arrestees, blacks just 23.0 percent. For drug abuse violations, whites accounted for 60.6 percent of the arrests, blacks for 36.4 percent. In fact, as mentioned previously, the only two categories in which black arrests exceeded white arrests were robbery and murder/nonnegligent manslaughter, in which African Americans accounted for 60.8 percent and 56.4 percent of the arrest totals, respectively.

Nearly one-half of all federal and state prison inmates are black, yet the proportion of blacks arrested for serious crimes doesn't approach that figure. What might explain this discrepancy? Do the statistics point to differences in the way the criminal justice system treats blacks and whites *after* arrest—perhaps in the way crimes are prosecuted and punished?

Christopher Lee Armstrong might answer that question in the affirmative. A police raid netted Armstrong, an African American, and four companions in their hotel room in a run-down section of Los Angeles one night in April 1992. Armstrong and the others would be charged with selling crack and using a firearm in connection with drug trafficking. The question was, would the men be charged in federal court, where the mandatory sentencing guidelines were severe, or in California state court, where the penalties were much more lenient?

Armstrong and his four African-American codefendants should not have been surprised when they found out their cases would be decided in federal court. After all, as the *Los Angeles Times* reported, not one white offender had been convicted of a crack cocaine offense in federal court in the Los Angeles metropolitan area since 1986, when Congress first enacted mandatory drug sentences. Of the 222 white defendants charged with crack cocaine offenses in Los Angeles from 1990 to 1992, all had been prosecuted in state court, thus enabling them to avoid the harsher sentences required under the federal sentencing mandates. The defendants in all 24 crack cocaine cases tried in federal court in Los Angeles during this period were African American.

This pattern occurs in other areas of the country as well. In more than half the federal court districts handling crack cases, only minorities have been prosecuted. A 1992 study revealed that no white defendants had been prosecuted federally on crack charges in 17 states and many cities, including Boston, Denver, Chicago,

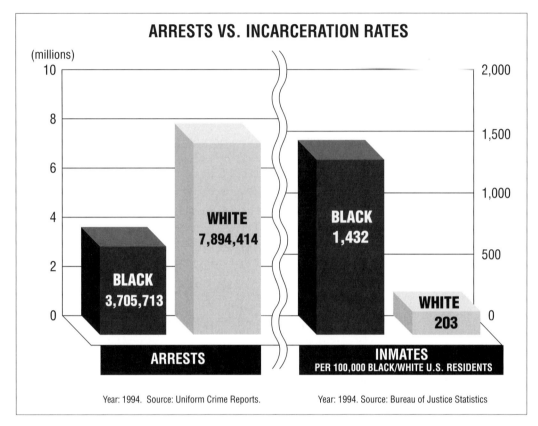

ARRESTS VS. INCARCERATION RATES

(millions)

BLACK
3,705,713

WHITE
7,894,414

BLACK
1,432

WHITE
203

ARRESTS

INMATES
PER 100,000 BLACK/WHITE U.S. RESIDENTS

Year: 1994. Source: Uniform Crime Reports.   Year: 1994. Source: Bureau of Justice Statistics

A comparison of arrests with incarceration rates reveals a disturbingly large racial gap.

Miami, and Dallas, in addition to Los Angeles. At the time of the study, out of hundreds of cases, only one white person had been convicted in federal court in California, two in Texas, three in New York, and two in Pennsylvania. Many people would argue, no doubt, that this is because most crack cocaine users are black. In fact, that is incorrect. According to federal surveys, most users of crack cocaine are white (a 1995 report put the figure at 52 percent).

The crack cocaine cases highlight a fact that all criminal justice professionals know well: prosecutors, like police officers and judges, have a certain amount of discretion in the performance of their duties. Just as a police officer who stops two drivers for speeding can let one go with a warning while giving the other a ticket, a prosecutor can choose, for example, to charge one man who has been involved in a fight with assault and another with the much more serious offense of attempted murder. Or a prosecutor can offer one defendant a plea-bargain deal—whereby the person pleads guilty to a lesser charge and receives a lesser penalty than he or she would have received if convicted at trial—and insist on taking another defendant who has committed the same crime to court on more serious charges. Some people would suggest that the abundance of blacks and the scarcity of whites charged in federal court for crack offenses evidences a tendency of prosecutors to use their discretion to the advantage of whites and the disadvantage of blacks.

Indeed, this is the argument Christopher Lee Armstrong and his codefendants made in appealing their convictions. They alleged that the U.S. Attorney's office in Los Angeles targeted its resources at minority communities and that the prosecutor engaged in "selective prosecution" based on race. Although Armstrong ultimately lost his appeal, in the case known as *Armstrong v. United States*, he and his lawyers did succeed in focusing attention on the issue of race-based prosecutorial strategies.

The Supreme Court has said that a prosecutor's discretion is "subject to constitutional constraints." Prosecutorial decisions, the Court has ruled, cannot *intentionally* be based on race. The rub, of course, is that it may be almost impossible to determine what is intentional discrimination and what is unintentional but nevertheless unequal treatment across races. In any event, the distinction probably isn't foremost in the minds of the people most affected. To an individual African-American defendant, the fact of unequal prosecutorial treatment is undoubtedly more important than the reasons for that unequal treatment.

The larger question confronting those who study race and criminal justice, however, is whether blacks as a group *are* actually disadvantaged by discretionary decisions at the prosecutorial stage, and if so, to what extent? An analysis of 800 cases tried in the Eighth Circuit Federal Court of Appeals sheds some light on that matter. The findings, reported in 1991, revealed that federal prosecutors routinely charged more black men than white men with offenses that called for mandatory sentences. It was also found that prosecutors were less inclined to offer plea bargains to black defendants, and that when plea bargains were offered, they were less generous than those offered to white defendants. As a result, the analysis revealed, blacks received sentences that were 49 percent longer than those of whites convicted of similar offenses. Black defendants could reduce their terms, the U.S. Sentencing Commission found, only if they turned in accomplices. (The U.S. Sentencing Commission is an advisory committee created by Congress in 1984 to develop federal sentencing guidelines that would, among other things, reduce sentencing disparity.)

Studies have also documented apparent bias in pretrial detention practices. Nationally, when compared with whites in the same category, unconvicted black defendants are more likely to be confined in jail while awaiting trial. A study of the justice system in Florida, for example, found that young, unemployed black men who were jailed on public order charges were three times more likely to be kept in jail pretrial than were unemployed white arrestees facing the same charges. The same pattern holds true for suspected juvenile offenders. In 1993, for example, white juvenile arrests exceeded black juvenile arrests by a minimum of 15 percent in every major offense category, but in every category a higher percentage of black juveniles than white juveniles were confined before the adjudication (resolution) of their cases.

Prosecutorial discretion also seems to work to the disadvantage of black defendants in murder cases, especially when the victim is white. In such cases, prosecutors request the death penalty 70 percent of the time, compared with just 32 percent of cases involving a white defendant and a white victim, and 15 percent of cases involving a black defendant and a black victim. The ratios are even more lopsided in southern states. For example, the Baldus Study, a comprehensive examination of more than 2,000 murder cases, found that in Georgia, prosecutors sought the death penalty in 70 percent of cases involving black defendants and white victims, but in just 19 percent of cases in which the victim was black and the defendant white. Other studies of other states have documented similar disparities as well.

If evidence suggests that prosecutorial discretion more frequently works to the disadvantage of African-American defendants than to the disadvantage of white defendants, racial disparities also arise at the next stage of the criminal justice process: sentencing.

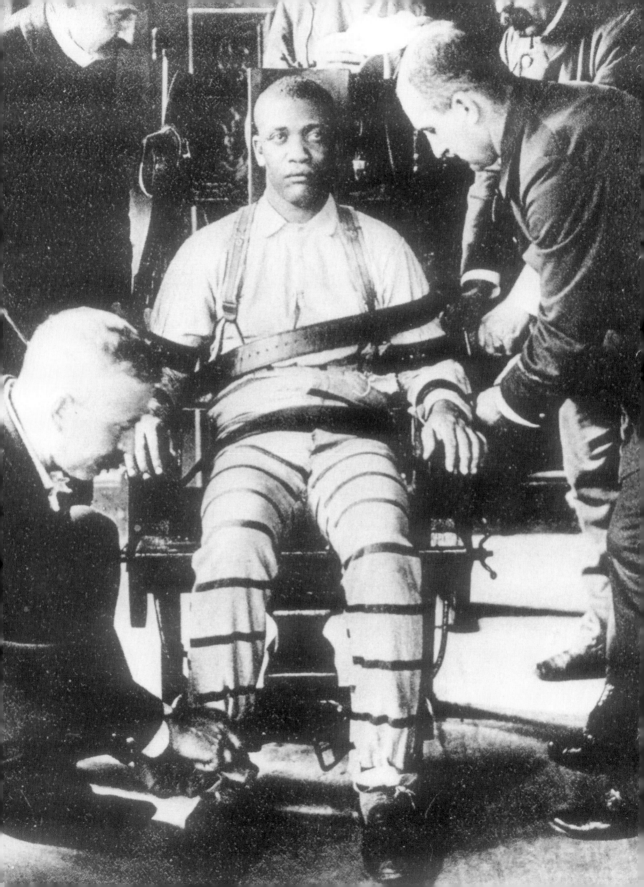

Disparity or Discrimination? Race and the Imposition of Sentence

An African American is strapped into the electric chair, circa 1920. Throughout American history, the death penalty has been applied more frequently to blacks than to whites.

In 1861 a portion of the Georgia Penal Code imposed a mandatory death penalty for the rape of a white woman by a black man and a prison sentence of 2 to 20 years for the same crime if committed by a white man. The rape of black women, by contrast, was punishable merely by "fine and imprisonment, 'at the discretion of the court.'"

Such legally mandated racial discrimination in the sentencing of criminals, which violates the basic principle that the law must apply equally to all groups, no longer exists in the United States. But that doesn't mean statutes that are apparently race-neutral haven't had an overwhelmingly negative impact on minorities. In recent years, two types of statutes—popularly referred to as "War on Drugs" and "three strikes and you're out" laws—have especially affected African Americans.

America's so-called War on Drugs began in the 1980s, when the dangers presented by illegal drugs seemed particularly acute. Cocaine abuse was rising, and crack, a cheap and exceedingly addictive form of the drug, had become available on the streets of the nation's major cities. Most disturbing, though, was an outbreak of deadly violence—much of it in poor urban neighborhoods—as rival drug gangs competed for a share of the market.

In response, Congress enacted a series of laws that prescribed severe penalties for drug offenders. One such law, the Omnibus Anti–Drug Abuse Act of 1986, included mandatory minimum sentences of five years' imprisonment—with no parole—even for first-time, nonviolent offenders convicted of selling or possessing with the intent to sell 500 grams of powder cocaine or 5 grams of crack cocaine. Congress toughened this law further in 1988. Having had some difficulty deciding what amount of the drug would indicate possession with intent to sell, the lawmakers opted to treat dealers, possessors, and conspirators of any kind the same. Under the law, mere possession of 5 grams of crack cocaine (about the weight of two pennies) triggers a mandatory sentence of five years in prison without the possibility of parole—the same penalty meted out for possession of 500 grams of powder cocaine. And the length of mandatory sentences increases with the amount possessed.

The 1988 law also changed conspiracy penalties. It allowed the same mandatory minimum sentence to apply to every participant in a drug ring, no matter how minor his or her role in the organization. Thus, a kingpin and a gofer would be treated as if they had dealt the same amount of drugs. If the organization had handled 50 pounds of cocaine, anyone in the organization could be subject to the penalties for selling that amount. Many states followed the federal government's lead, enacting laws that required mandatory prison sentences for possession of even relatively small amounts of illegal drugs. Beyond severely punishing drug-related offenses, the intent of these laws, according to various accounts, was to eliminate judges' discretion in sentencing drug offenders and to give prosecutors and law enforcement agents sufficient legal tools to go after high-level drug traffickers.

Not surprisingly, the new drug laws dramatically increased the number of jailed or imprisoned drug offenders—the figure went from 57,975 to 353,564 between 1983 and 1993—and the laws were one of the main reasons for the overall jump in America's incarceration rate. Setting aside the issues of whether it's appropriate to punish nonviolent offenders with long prison sentences and whether resources allocated to the construction of new prisons might have been better spent on drug rehabilitation programs, did the laws work as intended? That's a point of contention. Supporters cite the decline in the number of current illegal drug users (defined as anyone who has used an illicit drug in the previous month), from a high of 25.4 million (14.1 percent of the population) in 1979 to 12.0 million (5.8 percent of the population) by 1992. Critics note that the numbers slowly but steadily increased from 1993 to 1997 (the last year for which statistics are available) and point out that many variables other than the laws figure into rates of abuse. The epidemic of drug-related violence that plagued the inner cities in the early and mid-1980s is over, supporters observe; the reason, critics respond, is that the drug gangs' turf wars have largely been decided, and the victors are now firmly entrenched. Supporters say that the tough conspiracy penalties target drug kingpins, the people most responsible for distributing illegal drugs in America; critics wonder why so many low-level offenders and so few kingpins have actually been imprisoned.

Kemba Smith was certainly no drug kingpin, and in many ways she doesn't fit the typical image of a drug offender. Smith was a solidly middle-class college student, the daughter of two professionals—one an

William Armani Smith (above) will be 26 years old when his mother, Kemba Smith, is released from federal prison. Kemba Smith was sentenced to 24^1/$_2$ years, without the possibility of parole, for drug-related offenses.

accountant and chief financial officer, the other a high school teacher. And while there is no evidence that Smith ever used or sold drugs herself, she is serving a 24^1/$_2$-year term on drug-related charges at the federal women's penitentiary in Danbury, Connecticut. She has no chance of parole.

Smith's troubles began when, at the age of 19, she went off to attend college at Hampton University in Virginia. There she met Peter Michael Hall, a New Yorker originally from Jamaica who was eight years her senior. She fell in love with him. Only later did she discover that Hall was a drug dealer with several aliases. Throughout their relationship Hall abused her physically and verbally. Once Smith left him and returned to her parents in Richmond, Virginia, but eventually the two got back together. Knowing that Hall was a fugitive from justice, and pregnant with their child, Smith fled with him to the state of Washington.

By the time she summoned the courage to return home to her parents in Virginia once again, it was too late. Federal prosecutors had already begun building a case against Hall and others; she was among the others. Kemba Smith surrendered to federal authorities on September 1, 1994. Exactly one month later Peter Hall was found in an apartment in Seattle, Washington, dead from a gunshot wound to the head.

Although prosecutors conceded that there was no proof Smith had ever handled or used any cocaine, she faced a long list of charges, including obstruction of justice and money laundering, because of the help she had given Hall. On the advice of her attorney, she pleaded guilty to having conspired to distribute drugs.

At the sentencing hearing, her attorney argued that Smith had not acted under her own will, and two psychologists testified that her conduct was consistent with that of a battered woman—that is, she had acted under "coercion and duress." Smith's defense team hoped that this argument would persuade the judge to give her a reduced sentence.

But the prosecutor countered that although Smith did not directly sell the cocaine, she was aware of the activities of Hall's organization and had aided and abetted the conspiracy. Furthermore, contrary to the testimony of the psychologists, the prosecutor maintained that "the only explanation is she did it willingly for the love of Mr. Hall, not because she was afraid of him."

In pronouncing sentence on April 21, 1995, Judge Richard B. Kellam noted, "It's a sad mistake that she's made. It's a sad position that she's in, and she's placed her family in an even sadder position." But Kellam rejected Smith's claim of coercion and duress, stating that her involvement with Hall had continued for "too long a period of time" to make the claim believable. Once that had been decided, Judge Kellam had no choice: under federal drug laws, he had to impose lengthy sentences for the three charges of conspiracy, money laundering, and lying to authorities that Smith faced (all other charges had been dropped when she pleaded guilty). The actual sentences were 294 months for conspiracy, 60 months for money laundering, and 60 months for lying to authorities, the last two sentences to run concurrently with the first. "Putting [Smith] in incarceration will certainly not benefit her tremendously," Judge Kellam acknowledged. "The only purpose of it is [to be] a deterrent to others [so] that everyone knows that if they violate the law, they must pay the penalty."

In theory, as Judge Kellam indicated, everyone who violates drug laws will, if caught, pay the same tough, mandatory penalty. The federal and state legislators who passed America's antidrug laws no doubt felt that this would send a strong signal about the absolute unacceptability of drug trafficking and drug abuse, regardless of the offender's social standing. In practice, however, it seems that not everyone *has* faced the same penalties. If Kemba Smith, a middle-class college student from an intact family, in many ways doesn't represent society's image of a typical drug offender, in one way she is quite typical of the kind of person most likely to be sentenced to prison for drug offenses: she is black.

In the first five years after passage of the Omnibus Anti–Drug Abuse Act of 1986, African Americans accounted for more than 80 percent of the increase in drug offenders imprisoned in state and federal facilities. In state facilities during that period, the rate of black citizens incarcerated for drug offenses increased by 465.5 percent, compared to a 110.6 percent increase for whites.

In certain states, the disparity has been even more pronounced. In Minnesota, for example, the per capita increase in felony drug sentences between 1988 and 1994 was 1,096 percent for blacks, 71 percent for whites.

Such disparities have prompted more than one analyst to label America's War on Drugs a "war on African

Americans." Indeed, statistics on the number of blacks serving prison time for drug offenses are hard to reconcile with statistics on the number of blacks who actually use illegal drugs. According to the U.S. Sentencing Commission, 13 percent of all drug users are black. This is about the same proportion of blacks in the U.S. population. By contrast, 74 percent of all drug users are white. A greater proportion of blacks use crack cocaine, for which the criminal penalties are particularly severe, but whites still make up the majority of crack users (52 percent, compared with 38 percent blacks). Yet in 1993, a typical year, U.S. Sentencing Commission figures reveal that 88.3 percent of those sentenced federally for crack cocaine offenses were African American, while only 4.1 percent were white.

Like War on Drugs laws, so-called three-strikes statutes were designed both to target a certain kind of criminal (in this case, repeat serious- or violent-felony offenders) with lengthy prison sentences and to remove the discretion of judges, whose sentencing decisions across similar cases varied dramatically (and who were widely perceived to be too lenient). Generally the laws mandated that, upon conviction of a third serious or violent felony, the offender be sentenced to a long prison term—in many cases life—without parole. Between 1993 and 1995, the federal government and 24 states adopted some form of this legislation. Simple and equitable as the three-strikes laws sound on paper, they have, like the War on Drugs laws, given rise to significant disparities across race.

Georgia, for example, enacted a tough two-strikes sentencing scheme that imposes life imprisonment for a second drug offense. As of 1995, the state had invoked it against only 1 percent of white defendants facing a second drug conviction, but against more than 16 percent of eligible black defendants. The result is that 98.4 percent of those serving life sentences in Georgia under this provision are black.

Studies have shown that on average, blacks serve more time in prison than whites convicted of the same offenses.

In California, the first state to pass a three-strikes law, African Americans were imprisoned for a third offense at over 13 times the rate of whites during the first three years after the law took effect, according to the Justice Policy Institute in Washington, D.C. Blacks, who constitute only 7 percent of California's population and account for 20 percent of felony arrests, make up 43 percent of the state's more than 26,000 third-strike offenders, the institute reports. The more than 100 percent difference between felony arrests and third-strike sentences of African Americans is very difficult to explain—unless the law is being applied unequally.

Many commentators have questioned the manner in which three-strikes and antidrug laws are being applied nationwide. How is it, they wonder, that legislation intended to reduce sentencing disparity and target upper-level pushers and the most dangerous felons has ended up drawing within the net of social control the usual customers: minorities, the poor, and low-level offenders? A large part of the answer, it seems, is that far from reducing discretion in the way defendants are treated by the criminal justice system, these laws merely shifted it from judges at the sentencing phase to prosecutors at the charging phase. And prosecutors have charged a greater proportion of African Americans with offenses that call for long, mandatory prison sentences.

However, when judges retain discretion in sentencing decisions, blacks may also fare worse than whites convicted of similar offenses. Several studies have found this to be particularly true for less serious offenses, when judges must decide between probation and prison. A 1987 study by Cassia Spohn and colleagues found that in "borderline" cases, in which judges could impose either a lengthy probation sentence or a short prison sentence, they tended to sentence whites to probation and blacks to prison. A 1998 study that examined judicial decision-making in the cases of 223 adult offenders in Florida found that in "clear-cut" cases in which both the sentencing judge and the probation officer preparing the presentence report agreed that either a prison or probation term was called for, race did not influence the sentencing decision. However, when the researchers examined cases in which the characteristics of the defendant, case, and prior record did not clearly dictate prison over probation, judges were more apt to place whites on probation while sentencing blacks to jail.

When convicted of more serious crimes, offenders of all races are almost equally likely to receive a prison term. Statistics for 1992, for example, indicate that a fairly even percentage of whites, blacks, and Hispanics were sent to prison for various violent and nonviolent offenses. Still, in a majority of offense categories blacks, both male and female, received longer maximum sentences than their white counterparts at the time of initial sentencing for comparable offenses. In addition, blacks on average served more time before being released than did whites charged with the same offenses. In the "violent offenses" categories, for example, black males served, on average, 5 to 10 months more time in prison than did white males. When sentenced for the offense of murder, black females served on average 81 months before being released, whereas white females served 69 to 75 months.

What is driving sentencing decisions that result in comparable individuals of different racial backgrounds receiving different treatment? Is it simply the case that blacks are less likely, because of the impoverished communities in which they tend to live, to benefit from positive factors that judges consider in sentencing decisions, such as employment history, residential stability, or apparent "ties to the community"? Are blacks disadvantaged because most judges are white and of a higher socioeconomic class and might therefore have difficulty empathizing with them? Or are these sentences the outgrowth of something more disturbing, the historical (and socially reinforced) perception of blacks as dangerous, undeserving of civil liberties, and deserving of punishment? Basically the question involves a subtle, or perhaps not so subtle, distinction between disparity and discrimination. Disparity in criminal sentencing merely refers to the idea that individuals who commit the same or similar offenses receive different punishments once convicted. Disparate sentencing outcomes across race are possible even in the "absence of malice" on the part of the judicial authority making the sentencing decision. Discrimination, on the other hand, implies some level of intentional wrongdoing on the part of sentencing judges.

One might argue that unintentional but unwarranted disparity and intentional discrimination in sentencing are equally unacceptable. They do, after all, produce the same result—more severe treatment for a specific group of citizens. Yet the nation's highest court has ruled otherwise, and it has done so in a case involving the imposition of the law's most severe punishment, the death penalty.

Historically, the death penalty in America was applied disproportionally to blacks—especially in the southern states. Even after the repeal of laws that mandated racial discrimination in capital punishment, it was not difficult to discern a discriminatory purpose

Cocaine Controversy: Crack vs. Powder

In 1986, when Congress passed the federal Omnibus Anti–Drug Abuse Act, a key provision received little attention. It established mandatory minimum prison sentences of five years for anyone convicted of trafficking 5 grams of crack cocaine or 500 grams of powder cocaine. Two years later, in what was viewed as a minor technical correction to the original legislation, Congress made mere possession of those amounts of cocaine punishable by the mandatory sentences.

In the years since, the law has become the subject of much controversy. That is because crack cocaine is the drug of choice for many urban blacks, while the more expensive powder cocaine tends to be favored by more well-to-do white drug abusers. (Nearly 80 percent of those charged with possession of powder cocaine are white.) Thus, while many small-time, street-level black users of crack are receiving long prison sentences, whites—even dealers—caught with up to 99 times more powder cocaine (from which crack is produced) remain free.

There is no evidence that the lawmakers who passed the original legislation considered the disproportionate impact it would have on low-income minorities, much less that they intended to target blacks. Nevertheless, the law has had an undeniably disproportionate impact on blacks. The American Civil Liberties Union (ACLU) has called the policy "irrational, unwarranted, and discriminatory." Both the U.S. Sentencing Commission and the Criminal Division of the Department of Justice have recommended adjusting the 100-to-1 punishment disparity to 5-to-1 or 3-to-1. The Office of National Drug Control Policy favors a straight 1-to-1 ratio. If crack were treated like powder cocaine, experts estimate that the average sentence for convicted crack traffickers would be 47 months, as opposed to the 141 months currently imposed.

So far, however, Congress has refused to change the law. The Crack Cocaine Equitable Sentencing Act of 1995, a bill introduced by Representative Charles Rangel of New York, was defeated.

Whether the courts will intervene remains to be seen. In 1990, a Minnesota judge overturned that state's anti-crack law because it discriminated against African Americans. In the case of *Armstrong v. United States,* however, the U.S. Supreme Court rejected the claim of black defendants that the stiffer crack sentences were racially biased.

in the use of the death penalty. Between 1930 and 1964, for example, more than eight times as many blacks as whites—405 versus 48—were executed in the United States for the offense of rape. (The Supreme Court eventually outlawed the death penalty for rape in its 1977 *Coker v. Georgia* decision.) For other offenses blacks were also sentenced to death in greater proportions than whites.

Had William Henry Furman been a white man, he might not have received a death sentence. Around 2 A.M. on August 11, 1967, Furman broke into the Savannah, Georgia, house of a white man named William Micki and attempted to steal a television set. Micki heard him, however, and Furman fled. On the way out, Furman apparently tripped on an electric cord, and his gun accidentally discharged. The bullet passed through a closed door and struck Micki in the chest, killing him.

Furman's trial took only one day. The jury of 11 whites and 1 black found him guilty of murder and sentenced him to die in the electric chair. But attorneys for Furman appealed, and on January 17, 1972, the U.S. Supreme Court heard the case of *Furman v. Georgia*.

The attorney representing Furman, Anthony Amsterdam, argued that the death penalty violated the Eighth Amendment prohibition of cruel and unusual punishment because it was applied randomly. Some people were sentenced to die for armed robbery, while others convicted of the much more serious crime of murder faced only life imprisonment. Plus, statistical evidence suggested that race was a major factor in who received the death penalty. A black man convicted of raping a white woman, for example, stood a 38 percent

Evidence of racial inequality in capital punishment decisions helped convince Justice Potter Stewart (above) and four of his Supreme Court colleagues to overturn all death penalty laws in the 1972 Furman v. Georgia *ruling.*

chance of being sentenced to death, whereas a white man convicted of raping a white woman faced only a 0.5 percent chance. The entire process of choosing who would die was unfair, Amsterdam argued.

In a 5-4 decision delivered on June 29, 1972, the Supreme Court agreed. "[T]he [Eighth Amendment] cannot tolerate the infliction of a sentence of death under legal systems that permit this unique penalty to be so wantonly and freakishly imposed," wrote Justice Potter Stewart. By virtue of the Court's ruling, every death penalty statute in the 32 states that allowed capital punishment was declared unconstitutional.

State legislatures proceeded to rewrite their death penalty statutes in a way that would remove randomness and the taint of racial bias from sentencing decisions and hence pass constitutional muster. In 1976 the Supreme Court ruled that a number of states, including Georgia, Florida, and Texas, had found an acceptable formula. Their statutes required juries "to consider the [unique] circumstances of the crime and the criminal" before recommending sentence. This, the Court apparently believed, would eliminate not only random death penalty decisions but also racial discrimination in capital punishment.

The Court's optimism, statistics seem to indicate, was unfounded. Yet when another landmark death penalty case, *McCleskey v. Kemp*, came before the Court in 1987, the justices were unwilling to say that a pattern of racial disparity was grounds for constitutional concern.

In 1978 in Georgia, Warren McCleskey and three accomplices robbed a furniture store and fatally shot a white police officer. Although McCleskey denied being the shooter, he was convicted of first-degree murder and sentenced to death under what is termed the felony murder rule, which holds anyone involved in a felony crime responsible for any death that results in the course of that crime.

RACE AND THE DEATH PENALTY IN GEORGIA

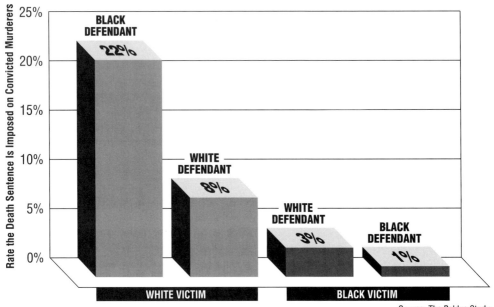

Source: The Baldus Study

In hearing the case of McCleskey v. Kemp, the Supreme Court accepted statistics showing that race continues to play a major role in who receives the death penalty. Nevertheless, the Court decided, a pattern of disparity is irrelevant to a particular case.

McCleskey appealed his sentence, and the Supreme Court agreed to hear the case. As with the *Furman v. Georgia* case, which had been decided 15 years earlier, *McCleskey v. Kemp* turned on the issue of race. Interestingly, one of McCleskey's lawyers was Anthony Amsterdam, who had also represented William Furman. Amsterdam noted that between 1973 and 1980, 17 people were charged with killing police officers in the Georgia county where Warren McCleskey committed his crime. Why, Amsterdam wondered, was McCleskey the only person sentenced to death? Could the reason be that he was black and the victim white?

Buttressing the argument were statistics presented to the Court from the Baldus Study. The study found that when all nonracial variables were taken into account, Georgia courts were 4.3 times more likely to hand out a death sentence when the victim was white, and in those cases a black defendant stood a far-greater chance than a white defendant (22 percent versus 8 percent) of receiving a death sentence. For blacks who killed blacks, a death sentence was imposed in only 1 percent of cases; for whites who killed blacks, in just 3 percent of cases.

Although they accepted these statistics as valid, the justices rejected McCleskey's appeal in a 5-4 decision. Even if a pattern of racial disparity in the administration of capital punishment could be demonstrated, the Court said that there was no proof the decision makers who sentenced McCleskey to death had acted with a "discriminatory purpose." Warren McCleskey was executed in Georgia's electric chair in September 1991.

Many observers are especially troubled by the *McCleskey* decision, as well as by the recent trend in appellate courts toward requiring that complainants prove "intentional harm" to prevail in claims of bias. Essentially the courts are saying that proving racial disparity—the standard that existed during the civil rights era—is no longer sufficient to obtain a legal remedy; proving intentional discrimination, an infinitely more difficult task, is now required.

It is undeniable that laws and criminal justice procedures have produced a significant, negative racial impact on African Americans. The fact that this impact occurs in the absence of any intent to discriminate serves as no consolation to those affected. Nor do court decisions that require proof of discrimination motivate lawmakers to devise solutions to the problem of racial disparity in criminal justice. Such decisions do, however, raise some disturbing questions about whose interests are and are not protected by the enactment of public laws. And in the minds of many people, the decisions are evidence that after nearly four centuries of unequal treatment of blacks, America is still unwilling to face its moral obligation to ensure that the law affects all groups equally.

A Troubling Future

If current trends continue, more than one in four African-American males born today will serve time in prison during their lifetimes. A criminal record, in turn, reduces employment opportunities, decreases marriage chances, and may lead to the loss of civil rights. Ultimately this could produce a never-ending cycle of poverty, social disintegration, and crime.

In 1999 the Bureau of Justice Statistics estimated that if current trends continued, 16.2 percent of all African Americans would serve a prison term at some point in their life. (For whites the estimate was only 2.5 percent.) More troubling still was the outlook for black males: fully 28 percent were projected to do prison time. The enormity of this situation can hardly be overstated: unless there is a change in course, more than one of every four black males born today will eventually wind up behind bars.

Leaving aside for now the social implications of imprisoning such a large proportion of blacks, what do these figures say about the criminal justice system? Can a system that yields an incarceration rate more than six times higher for African Americans than for whites possibly be fair?

Statistics, of course, don't tell the full story. And, for the most part, the commonly reported statistics—rates of offending by race—oversimplify complex issues of race, crime, and punishment. The frequency with which these issues resurface, and the intensity of the reactions they produce in such cases as the Rodney King beating and the murder trial of O. J. Simpson, reflect a controversial past and suggest an unstable and troubling future. While reactions to such cases may appear temporary, the racial overtones surrounding the cases raise fundamental questions about whether the American system of justice will ever be fair toward everyone or whether race will always be a factor in the way people are treated under the law.

Whatever else can be said about the Simpson case, it brought to the forefront the strong influence of race on perceptions of justice and injustice. It revealed to some, while reinforcing for others, a belief widespread among minorities: that the system is tilted against people of color. The fact that many whites remain unwilling to accept the criminal verdict—coming as it did from a predominantly minority jury—hints at the depth and complexity of the problem.

Similarly, the controversy over the prevalence and legitimacy of race-based profiling in law enforcement reveals the breadth of the racial gulf. Indeed, it might be argued that 130 years after the abolition of slavery, America is still debating the question of whether blacks should receive all the rights and protections their white neighbors enjoy. Recent court decisions have in effect left individual minorities in the uncomfortable position of being presumed guilty—and hence of being sub-jected to extra police scrutiny.

A 1999 decision by the U.S. Court of Appeals for the Second Circuit (*Brown v. City of Oneonta*) upheld the legality of police stopping and questioning *every* black male in Oneonta, New York, in connection with a burglary investigation. The criminal case began in 1992, when an elderly white victim of a nighttime bur-glary told the police that, while it had been dark and she had not seen the face of the intruder, she could tell from his arms and hands that he was black, and because he had moved quickly she thought he was young. The woman also believed that the intruder had cut his hand with a knife he was carrying. Based on this information, the police obtained a list of all black male students at a nearby college campus and began to question them. They also questioned all black men who were permanent residents of the town. The court ruled that the stops—more than 500 in all—were not racially discriminatory because race wasn't the only element in the description upon which the police were acting. Nevertheless, it's hard to imagine that under similar circumstances the courts would countenance the questioning of all *white* males in an area. The case, in which the presumption of innocence seems to have been suspended for all black males, led a *New York Times* journalist to coin the phrase "breathing while black" to describe the reason for the extra police scrutiny.

The courts have similarly paved the way for the police use of race-based profiles for drug-interdiction efforts on the highways. In 1989, in the case of *United States v. Sokolow*, the Court upheld the police use of profiles generally. In the 1996 case *Whren v. United States*, the Court ruled that if otherwise legally supported, a police officer's motives for making a traffic stop are irrelevant to the validity of the stop. Thus stops and searches for drugs based on race can be effectively concealed under the pretext of a mere traffic violation.

In its 1997 decision in the case of *Maryland v. Wilson*, the Court ruled that as a matter of "routine," police may demand that all passengers exit a vehicle when the driver is stopped for a traffic violation. And in April 1999, in the case of *Wyoming v. Houghton*, the Court ruled that the belongings of such passengers can be searched without a warrant even if it is the driver, not the passenger, who is suspected of criminal activity.

While at first glance the *Wilson* and *Houghton* rulings appear to have nothing to do with race, a closer look at police practices indicates otherwise. In 1995, for example, Maryland state troopers reported conducting 533 stops along a particular stretch of highway. Among those stopped were 409 black motorists, compared with only 97 whites. Drugs were found in 33 percent of stopped cars containing black motorists, and in 22 percent of cars containing white motorists. Although this 11 percent difference might appear to validate the use of racial profiling, it must be noted that the police interfered with the liberty of more than four times as many innocent blacks as innocent whites (270 versus 64).

Rather than thinking of blacks as individuals, each entitled to the protection of constitutional and civil rights, many police officers seem to feel that since blacks as a group commit a disproportionate amount of crime, racial profiling is simply a tool of good police work. To law-abiding blacks, however, "fitting the description" or having been born with "the color of suspicion" is never a justification for being subjected to unwarranted police stops.

In addition to denying blacks the "blessings of liberty" laid out in the preamble to the Constitution, the increased police scrutiny under which African Americans often find themselves, coupled with socioeconomic conditions conducive to crime, greatly increases their potential exposure to the criminal justice system. Given the retributive nature of current criminal justice policy, exposure to the system increasingly means incarceration and the staggering social disruption that it brings.

Ex-convicts suffer greatly diminished job prospects, not only because employers are generally reluctant to hire people with felony records but also because some jurisdictions restrict felons' rights to hold a driver's license and be bonded or licensed for various professions. In the absence of opportunities to make a living through legitimate means, many convicts who would otherwise not be inclined to commit further criminal acts after

their release from prison might once again turn to crime. (Obviously, a certain percentage of ex-convicts would be repeat offenders under any circumstances.) Even those who don't reoffend face a future that includes a dramatically higher likelihood of living in poverty.

But it is not just the convicts themselves who are affected. The removal to prison of large numbers of young African-American males creates a shortage of marriage partners for black women. How significant might this shortage be? A 1997 Urban Institute report estimated that some areas saw 1.3 percent of all black males between the ages of 16 and 34 arrested and sentenced to prison in one year, and for drug offenses alone. One result is more women raising children by themselves—and, chances are, raising those children in

Young, African American, and a city dweller: at risk from social conditions and criminal justice policies?

poverty. And both poverty and single-parent families are risk factors for juvenile crime. The scarcity of men in a neighborhood may also increase juvenile crime by creating easier targets and by removing the informal social controls that men tend to provide.

The number of African-American women in prison has increased dramatically as well, primarily as the result of the War on Drugs. In the 10-year period beginning in 1986, the number of black women sentenced to state prisons on drug-related charges increased by 828 percent. Two-thirds of these women, like Kemba Smith, have children under the age of 18. This is especially troubling. Nine out of 10 children with fathers in prison live with their mothers, who frequently raise the children alone. While that increases a child's risk of delinquency and crime, the situation is much worse when mothers are imprisoned. In that case only one in four children live with their fathers. Sometimes children whose mothers are in prison are left to the care of grandparents, siblings, aunts, and uncles. Although such arrangements can be problematic, they are often preferable to the foster care system. Data suggest that youth who come to the attention of child welfare authorities are 67 times more likely than others to become involved in crime.

Thus, America's large-scale incarceration of blacks may only be perpetuating—if not actually worsening—the crime problem. Among the very group that already suffers most from poverty, community disorganization, and family disruption—factors that increase crime rates—massive imprisonment creates more poverty, more community disorganization, and more family disruption. To use a hackneyed phrase, it is a vicious circle.

Many people would argue that while regrettable, this situation is unavoidable. Crime, after all, must be punished or society will break down. And ultimately the fault for the "black crime problem"—along with any possible solution—lies exclusively within the

African-American community itself.

This argument ignores several key points. First of all, blacks, as we have seen, suffer disparities at each stage of the criminal justice process: law enforcement, prosecution, and sentencing. Though they commit a disproportionate amount of crime, they receive demonstrably harsher treatment by the criminal justice system, and this unequal treatment—in addition to raising fundamental concerns about the system's impartiality—may indirectly lead to more crime. Second, when laws are wreaking havoc on one racial or ethnic group in particular—as are the nation's drug laws—it is appropriate to question the basic fairness of those laws. For example, given the obvious racial impact the statute has had, is it fair to continue punishing the possession of crack cocaine 100 times more severely than the possession of powder cocaine, from which crack is made? Is crack really 100 times more dangerous? Another, more practical, question also arises: Is the solution worse than the problem? What poses a greater risk to society—abuse of crack cocaine or the imprisonment of tens of thousands of nonviolent offenders, with the accompanying social disruption?

It is a sad irony that after the prolonged struggle and sacrifice blacks undertook to win the right to vote—one of the most coveted civil rights—large numbers of African Americans are again disenfranchised. As a result of felony convictions, one out of every seven black men is currently or permanently barred from voting.

It remains to be seen whether that setback can itself be reversed. One thing is certain, however. The problem of race and crime—rooted as it is in American history, social structure, and criminal justice—is one of the most difficult and perplexing issues that America faces as a new century begins. The consequences of not confronting the problem and working to find solutions could one day prove catastrophic.

Bibliography

Baldus, D.; G. Woodworth; and C. Pulaski. *Equal Justice and the Death Penalty. A Legal and Empirical Analysis.* Boston: Northeastern University Press, 1990.

Canada, G. *Fist Stick Knife Gun.* Boston: Beacon Press, 1995.

Cole, D. *No Equal Justice.* New York: The Free Press, 1999.

Cose, E. *The Rage of a Privileged Class.* New York: HarperCollins Publishers, 1993.

DiMascio, W. *Seeking Justice.* New York: The Edna McConnell Clark Foundation, 1995.

Ginzburg, R. *One Hundred Years of Lynchings.* Baltimore: The Black Classic Press, 1988.

Hacker, A. *Two Nations: Black and White, Separate, Hostile, Unequal.* New York: Ballantine Books, 1992.

Mann, C. *Unequal Justice.* Bloomington: Indiana University Press, 1993.

McIntyre, C. *Criminalizing a Race.* Queens, N.Y.: Kayode Publications, Ltd., 1993.

Miller, J. *Search and Destroy.* New York: Cambridge University Press, 1996.

Myrdal, G. *An American Dilemma.* New York: Harper Brothers, 1944.

Owens, C., and J. Bell. *Blacks and Criminal Justice.* Lexington, Mass.: D.C. Heath and Company, 1977.

Russell, K. *The Color of Crime.* New York: New York University Press, 1998.

Sampson, R., and W. J. Wilson. "Toward a Theory of Race, Crime and Urban Inequality." In *Crime and Inequality.* Edited by J. Hagan and R. Peterson. Stanford, Calif.: Stanford University Press, 1995.

Tonry, M. *Malign Neglect.* New York: Oxford University Press, 1995.

Walker, S.; C. Spohn; and M. DeLone. *The Color of Justice.* New York: Wadsworth Publishing Company, 1996.

Wilson, J. *The Moral Sense.* New York: The Free Press, 1993.

Wilson, W. J. *The Truly Disadvantaged.* Chicago: University of Chicago Press, 1990.

Index

Index

DELORES D. JONES-BROWN is currently an assistant professor at John Jay College of Criminal Justice, City University of New York, and a fellow with the National Development Research Institutes, Inc., in New York City. She is a former research fellow at Teachers College, Columbia University, and a former assistant prosecutor for Monmouth County, New Jersey. She received a law degree from Rutgers University School of Law in Newark, and she holds a masters and a doctorate in Criminal Justice from Rutgers as well as an undergraduate degree in Sociology and the Administration of Law from Howard University in Washington, D.C. Dr. Jones-Brown has written several articles and book chapters on various aspects of race and the administration of justice in the United States. She lives with her family in Freehold, New Jersey.

AUSTIN SARAT is William Nelson Cromwell Professor of Jurisprudence and Political Science at Amherst College, where he also chairs the Department of Law, Jurisprudence and Social Thought. Professor Sarat is the author or editor of 23 books and numerous scholarly articles. Among his books are *Law's Violence, Sitting in Judgment: Sentencing the White Collar Criminal,* and *Justice and Injustice in Law and Legal Theory.* He has received many academic awards and held several prestigious fellowships. In addition, he is a nationally recognized teacher and educator whose teaching has been featured in the *New York Times,* on the *Today* show, and on National Public Radio's *Fresh Air.*

Picture Credits